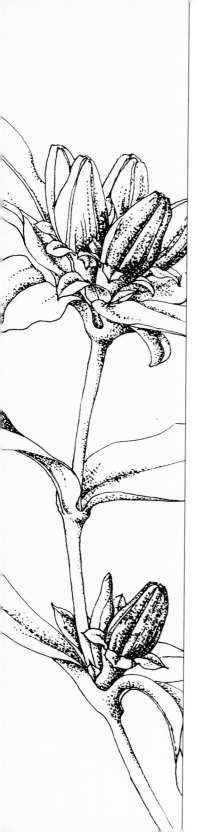

WILDFLOWERS
OF MAINE,
NEW HAMPSHIRE,
AND VERMONT

IN COLOR

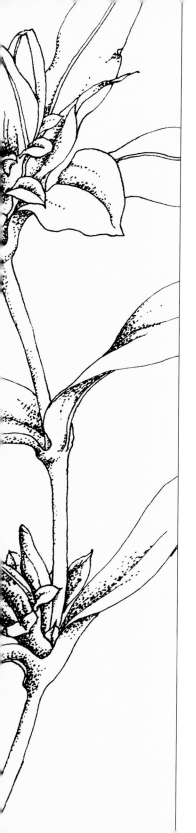

WILDFLOWERS OF MAINE, NEW HAMPSHIRE, AND VERMONT

IN COLOR

Alan E. Bessette
Arleen Rainis Bessette
William K. Chapman
Valerie Conley Chapman

Botanical Drawings by
Philippa Brown

Syracuse University Press

First Edition 2000
00 01 02 03 04 05   6 5 4 3 2 1

All photographs courtesy of the authors.

The paper used in this publication meets the minimum requirements
of American National Standard for Information Sciences
—Permanence of Paper for Printed Library Materials,
ANSI Z39.48–984. ∞™

Library of Congress Cataloging-in-Publication Data

   Wildflowers of Maine, New Hampshire, and Vermont in color /
      Alan E. Bessette...{et al.}—1st ed.
            p.   cm.
   ISBN 0–8156–2803–X (alk. paper).
   — ISBN 0–8156–0586–2 (pbk.: alk. paper)
   1. Wild flowers—Maine—Identification.
   2. Wild flowers—New Hampshire—Identification.
   3. Wild flowers—Vermont—Identification.
   4. Wild flowers—Maine—Pictorial works.
   5. Wild flowers—New Hampshire—Pictorial works.
   6. Wild flowers—Vermont—Pictorial works.
   I. Bessette, Alan.

   QK164.W56   2000
   582.13'0974—DC21
   99–046641

Manufactured in Hong Kong through Cristina Lazar

Book design by Cristina Lazar
grafika@well.com

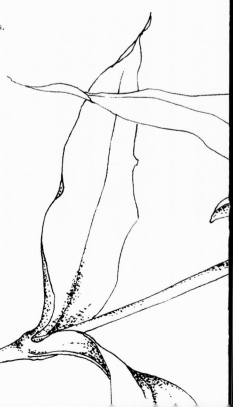

To our parents

❦

CONTENTS

ACKNOWLEDGMENTS

The authors wish to acknowledge the many people who have contributed valuable time and effort on behalf of this book. The *Revised Checklist of New York State Plants* by Richard S. Mitchell and Gordon C. Tucker served as our primary reference source for nomenclature and terminology. We thank Philippa Brown for providing the botanical drawings. We are especially grateful to Dr. Robert Mandel and his staff at Syracuse University Press, who made this book possible.

HOW TO USE THIS GUIDE

We have prepared this field guide to make identifying unfamiliar flowers as easy a process as possible. By following the simple procedure described below, you will be able to identify the wildflowers described in this book in a matter of minutes simply by making choices having to do with a few easily differentiated characteristics.

The first characteristic to consider is *color*. Is the flower white, the color that is in reality the reflection of all other colors? After white, the other choices are the colors of the rainbow. This guide follows the example of nature and lists those colors in the same order that they are displayed across the sky after a storm, beginning with red and continuing through violet. Within the spectrum, the color that is somewhat problematic and causes the greatest concern is purple. Purple flowers with a predominant bluish cast have been included in the blue to violet category. All the species whose color appears to have been visibly influenced by any degree or shade of pink-to-red pigmentation have been included in the pink-to-red category. The final color choice encompasses the darkest colors to be found on flowers, those ranging from deep purple to brown. Occasionally a flower is found that is such a dark shade of purple that it first appears to be nearly black. However, we are not aware of any truly black wildflower.

One final note on identifying flower colors: In some flowers the color of the petals or the petal-like parts differs from the color of the disc or center of the bloom. In such cases, we have assigned that species to a color category according to the color of the petals.

After you ascertain the color of a wildflower, your next task is to examine the *physical structure of the flower*. Is the flower radially symmetrical or nearly so? Radially symmetrical flowers have petals or petal-like parts that extend outward from the center of the flower more or less evenly in all directions, as in the daisy for example. (The term "petals or petal-like parts" is used throughout this guide to refer to any floral—usually colorful—parts that appear to be a petal, even though technically these parts may be sepals, modified bracts, etc.) If a flower is radially symmetrical, you should then count the number of petals or petal-like parts. The possible categories range from 3 to 7 or more petals or petal-like parts. A few species, such as goldthread or bloodroot, typically exhibit variation in the number of petals per bloom. In these cases we have relied on personal experience in assigning such species to the category that is most appropriate.

Following the 5 categories of radially symmetrical flowers is the final possible selection, a catch-all classification for any wildflowers not fitting into the previous categories. Flowers in this grouping do not appear to be radially symmetrical. They may have fewer than 3 petals or petal-like parts; or flowers that are minute, filamentous, tubular with no or uneven petal-like lobes; or with no obvious petals or petal-like parts. If a flower is tubular to dish-shaped with a number of conspicuous, symmetrical, petal-like lobes, then that species will be found in the radially symmetrical category. If the flower is tubular but the lobes (or "teeth") are either unequal in size and shape or minute, then that species will be found in the asymmetrical category.

After you determine the color and structure of the flower, your next task is to examine the leaves. The *leaf arrangement* on the plant should fall into one of the following categories: (1) aquatic *, (2) leaves lacking, (3) leaves basal, (4) leaves alternate, (5) leaves opposite or whorled.

In some species leaf arrangement may include two categories, such as having both basal and alternate leaves on the same plant. In these cases the plant is assigned to a category according to which leaves appear to be the more prominent. You should also take leaf arrangement to mean the way the leaves would appear at first glance to the average person encountering the plant for the first time. For example, several species have trailing or subterranean stems that put up leaves and flowers at intervals. If the leaves of such plants appear basal, then that is the category in which they are included.

---

*Although "aquatic" is not a true leaf arrangement, it is a useful category for simplifying the identification process.

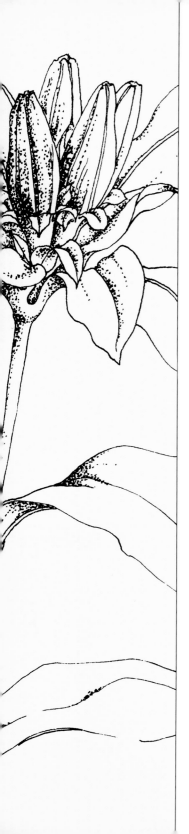

PART ONE

WHITE FLOWERS

❧

FLOWERS SYMMETRICAL, WITH 3 PETALS OR PETAL-LIKE PARTS

LEAVES BASAL, SIMPLE

Arrowhead, Wapato
• *Sagittaria latifolia* Willd.
• Water-plantain family **Alismataceae**
FLOWERING SEASON: July–August. FLOWERS: white with a yellow center, in whorls of 3 on a loosely flowered upright stem, about 1¼" (3.1 cm) wide, with 3 rounded petals. PLANT: aquatic, 4–36" (10–90 cm) tall; leaves basal, erect, simple, arrowhead-shaped, long-stalked, margin entire, green. HABITAT: shallow water. COMMENTS: several other species of *Sagittaria*, some with very narrow leaves, also occur in New York.

LEAVES WHORLED, SIMPLE

White Trillium
• *Trillium grandiflorum* (Michx.) Salisb.
• Lily family **Liliaceae**
FLOWERING SEASON: late April through May. FLOWER: white, becoming pink just before wilting, solitary and terminal on a tall erect stalk, about 3" (7.5 cm) wide, with 3 large, evenly whorled petals; petals ovate with a tapering, pointed tip, often slightly recurved. PLANT: 8–18" (20–45 cm) tall; leaves 3, in a whorl at the base of the flower stalk, simple, ovate with a tapering, pointed tip and an entire margin, practically stalkless, green. HABITAT: woodlands. COMMENTS: the name trillium refers to three, the number of leaves, sepals, and petals.

Painted Trillium
• *Trillium undulatum* Willd.
• Lily family **Liliaceae**
FLOWERING SEASON: May. FLOWER: white with crimson veins around the center, solitary and terminal on an erect stalk; about 2" (5 cm) wide, with 3 evenly whorled petals, petals lance-shaped with a tapering, pointed tip. PLANT: 8–24" (20–60 cm) tall; leaves 3, in a whorl at the base of the flower stalk, simple, ovate with a tapering, pointed tip and an entire margin, short-stalked, green. HABITAT: woodlands.

Nodding Trillium
• *Trillium cernuum* L.
• Lily family **Liliaceae**
FLOWERING SEASON: mid-May to mid-June. FLOWER: white, solitary and terminal on a drooping stalk characteristically oriented below the leaves, with 3 evenly whorled petals, petals about 1" (2.5 cm) long, broadly lance-shaped, deeply recurved. PLANT: 8–20" (20–50 cm) tall; leaves 3, in a whorl at the base of the flower stalk, simple, broadly ovate with a pointed tip and an entire margin, stalkless or nearly so, green. HABITAT: moist woodlands, wooded swamps.

FLOWERS SYMMETRICAL, WITH 4 PETALS OR PETAL-LIKE PARTS

LEAVES ALTERNATE, SIMPLE

Garlic Mustard
• *Alliaria petiolata* (Bieb.) Cav. and Grande
• Mustard family **Brassicaceae**
FLOWERING SEASON: May. FLOWERS: white, few to several in a terminal cluster, about 5⁄16" (8 mm) wide, cross-shaped, with 4 narrowly oval petals. PLANT: 1–3' (30–90 cm) tall; leaves alternate, simple, heart-shaped to triangular, margin coarsely toothed, green; seed pods 1–2" (2.5–5 cm) long, very slender. HABITAT: roadsides, waste areas, fields, and woodlands. COMMENTS: crushed leaves have a garlic-like odor.

Arrowhead, Wapato / *Sagittaria latifolia*

White Trillium / *Trillium grandiflorum*

Painted Trillium / *Trillium undulatum*

Nodding Trillium / *Trillium cernuum*

Garlic Mustard / *Alliaria petiolata*

Field Pennycress
- *Thlaspi arvense* L.
- Mustard family **Brassicaceae**

FLOWERING SEASON: early May to mid-June. FLOWERS: white, several to many in a terminal cluster, about 1/16" (2 mm) wide, cross-shaped, with 4 oval petals. PLANT: 6–18" (15–46 cm) tall; leaves alternate, simple, lance-shaped, often clasping the stem, margin toothed, green; seed pods about 3/8" (1 cm) long, oval with a notched tip, flattened. HABITAT: fields and waste places.

Wild Peppergrass
- *Lepidium virginicum* L.
- Mustard family **Brassicaceae**

FLOWERING SEASON: mid-May to July. FLOWERS: white, many in slender terminal clusters, about 1/16" (1.6 mm) wide, cross-shaped, with 4 oval petals. PLANT: 6–24" (15–60 cm) tall; leaves alternate and basal, simple, upper leaves lance-shaped, margin sharply toothed or entire, basal leaves obovate with tiny lobes along the stalk, margin toothed, green; seed pods about 5/8" (1.6 cm) long, nearly round, notched. HABITAT: fields and roadsides. COMMENTS: fieldcress, *Lepidium campestre*, has oblong to paddle-shaped basal leaves and narrowly arrowhead-shaped stem leaves.

Sea-rocket
- *Cakile edentula* (Bigel.) Hook.
- Mustard family **Brassicaceae**

FLOWERING SEASON: July-August. FLOWERS: white to pale purple, few in a terminal cluster, about 1/4" (6 mm) wide, cross-shaped, with 4 oval petals. PLANT: 8–12" (20–30 cm) tall; leaves alternate, simple, lance-shaped, margin unevenly toothed, green; seed pods 1/2–3/4" (1.3–1.9 cm) long, 2-sectioned, upper section slightly larger, ovoid. HABITAT: coastal sandy soil, also along Lake Erie.

Large Cranberry
- *Vaccinium macrocarpon* Ait.
- Heath family **Ericaceae**

FLOWERING SEASON: mid-June through July. FLOWERS: white to pinkish white with a brownish cone-shaped center, many, axial, about 5/16" (8 mm) wide, tubular with 4 narrow, deeply recurved, petal-like lobes. PLANT: woody, branched, trailing; leaves alternate, simple, oblong, small, margin entire, green; fruit an acidic, ovoid red berry. HABITAT: bogs, fen meadows.

Canadian Mayflower
- *Maianthemum canadense* Desf.
- Lily family **Liliaceae**

FLOWERING SEASON: late May to late June. FLOWERS: white, up to 20 in an oval terminal cluster 1–2" (2.5–5 cm) long, individual flowers about 3/16" (5 mm) wide, with 4 oblong petal-like parts. PLANT: 2–7" (5–17.5 cm) tall; leaves usually 2, alternate, simple, somewhat heart-shaped, margin entire, green, glossy. HABITAT: woodlands. COMMENTS: unusual in that most members of the lily family have perianth parts in multiples of 3. Also known as the false or wild lily-of-the-valley.

Sea-rocket / *Cakile edentula*

Large Cranberry / *Vaccinium macrocarpon*

Wild Peppergrass / *Lepidium virginicum*

Field Pennycress / *Thlaspi arvense*

Canadian Mayflower / *Maianthemum canadense*

LEAVES ALTERNATE, COMPOUND OR DEEPLY DIVIDED

Cut-leaf Toothwort

•*Cardamine concatenata* (Michx.) Schwein
•Mustard family **Brassicaceae**
FLOWERING SEASON: late April to mid-May. FLOWERS: white, few to several, in a terminal cluster, about ⅝" (1.6 cm) wide, cross-shaped, with 4 oval petals. PLANT: 8–15" (20–37.5 cm) tall; leaves alternate, deeply divided, margin coarsely toothed, green; seed pods 1–1½" (2.5–3.8 cm) long, slender, spreading. HABITAT: woodlands. COMMENTS: two-leaf toothwort, *Cardamine diphylla*, which blooms just after the cut-leaf toothwort, has leaves with 3 broad ovate divisions.

Watercress

•*Rorippa nasturtium-aquaticum* (L.) Hayek
•Mustard family **Brassicaceae**
FLOWERING SEASON: June into August. FLOWERS: white, several in terminal clusters, about ³⁄₁₆" (5 mm) wide, cross-shaped, with 4 oval petals. PLANT: aquatic; leaves alternate, pinnately compound with 3 to 9 segments, margins uneven, green; seed pods about 1" (2.5 cm) long, slender, long-stalked, spreading. HABITAT: in brooks, streams, and drainage ditches.

LEAVES OPPOSITE OR WHORLED, SIMPLE

Bunchberry

•*Cornus canadensis* L.
•Dogwood family **Cornaceae**
FLOWERING SEASON: June. FLOWERHEAD: white with a greenish center, about 1" (2.5 cm) wide, rimmed by 4 to 6 large white petal-like bracts; individual flowers tiny, greenish, with 4 minute petals. PLANT: 3–9" (7.5–22.5 cm) tall; leaves whorled, simple, ovate with a pointed tip, margin entire, green; fruit a ¼" (6 mm) wide "bunched cluster" of smooth bright red berries. HABITAT: woodlands.

Red Osier Dogwood

•*Cornus sericea* L.
•Dogwood family **Cornaceae**
FLOWERING SEASON: mid-May to mid-June. FLOWERS: dull white, many in flat-topped clusters 1½"–2" (4–5 cm) wide; individual flowers small, with 4 narrow petals. PLANT: shrub, 3–6' (1–1.8 m) tall; leaves opposite, simple, lance-shaped with a pointed tip, margin entire, olive-green; bark bright maroon-red; fruit white with a black "eye." HABITAT: moist meadows.

Sweet-scented Bedstraw

•*Galium triflorum* Michx.
•Madder family **Rubiaceae**
FLOWERING SEASON: June-July. FLOWERS: white to greenish white, many in 3-branched terminal and axial clusters, tiny, corolla with 4 sharply pointed, petal-like lobes. PLANT: 1–3' (30–90 cm) tall; leaves whorled in groups of 6 on a smooth stalk, simple, narrowly oval, margin entire, green. HABITAT: fields and waste areas. COMMENTS: goosegrass, *Galium aparine*, has a spiny stem, rough leaves, and small clusters of axial flowers.

Woodruff

•*Galium odoratum* (L.) Scop.
•Madder family **Rubiaceae**
FLOWERING SEASON: mid-May to mid-June. FLOWERS: white, several in flat-topped terminal clusters, about ¼" (6 mm) wide, tubular with 4 sharp, petal-like lobes. PLANT: 4–7" (10–17.5 cm) tall; leaves in 3 or 4 whorls of about 8, simple, lance-shaped, margin entire, green. HABITAT: waste areas, meadows, and open woodlands. COMMENTS: this herb is used to flavor May wine.

Bunchberry / *Cornus canadensis*

Watercress / *Rorippa nasturtium-aquaticum*

Cut-leaf Toothwort / *Cardamine concatenata*

Sweet-scented Bedstraw / *Galium triflorum*

Woodruff / *Galium odoratum*

Red Osier Dogwood / *Cornus sericea*

Partridge-berry, Twin-berry

- *Mitchella repens* L.
- Madder family **Rubiaceae**

FLOWERING SEASON: late June through July. **FLOWERS:** white, in terminal pairs, up to ½" (1.3 cm) long, tubular with 4 pointed and often recurved, petal-like lobes. **PLANT:** prostrate; leaves opposite on 6–12" (15–30 cm) long stems, simple, nearly round, margin entire, green, often with whitish veining, evergreen. **HABITAT:** woodlands. **COMMENTS:** the bright red berries are edible but bland.

LEAVES OPPOSITE, COMPOUND

Virgin's-bower

- *Clematis virginiana* L.
- Crowfoot family **Ranunculaceae**

FLOWERING SEASON: late July through August. **FLOWERS:** white, several in showy axial clusters, about 1" (2.5 cm) wide, with 4 narrowly oblong, petal-like sepals and numerous, prominent thread-like stamens. **PLANT:** a climbing vine up to 10' (3 m) long; leaves opposite, with 3 lance-shaped occasionally lobed leaflets, margins unevenly toothed, green. **HABITAT:** open woodlands, hedgerows, and wooded swamps. **COMMENTS:** this species produces showy clusters of plumed seeds.

FLOWERS SYMMETRICAL, WITH 5 PETALS OR PETAL-LIKE PARTS

LEAVES BASAL, SIMPLE

Spathulate-leaved Sundew

- *Drosera intermedia* Hayne
- Sundew family **Droseraceae**

FLOWERING SEASON: July into August. **FLOWERS:** white, several, in a slender terminal cluster, about ¼" (6 mm) wide, with 5 oblong petals. **PLANT:** 3–8" (7.5–20 cm) tall; leaves basal, simple, spoon-shaped with long stalks, upper surface covered with reddish glandular hairs with a sticky, syrup-like coating, margin entire, green. **HABITAT:** bogs, fens, and wet sand. **COMMENTS:** a carnivorous plant that uses its sticky hairs to entrap insects. Round-leaved sundew, *Drosera rotundifolia*, has nearly round leaves, while thread-leaved sundew, *D. filiformis* has long, narrow, thread-like leaves.

Round-leaf Pyrola, Shinleaf

- *Pyrola americana* Sweet
- Health family **Ericaceae**

FLOWERING SEASON: late June through July. **FLOWERS:** white, several to many on a spike-like terminal cluster, about ¾" (1.9 cm) wide, with 5 rounded petals, nodding. **PLANT:** 6–20" (15–50 cm) tall; leaves basal, simple, nearly round, margin minutely toothed, green. **HABITAT:** woodlands.

One-sided Pyrola, One-sided Wintergreen

- *Orthilia secunda* (L.) House
- Heath family **Ericaceae**

FLOWERING SEASON: July. **FLOWERS:** white, several on a one-sided terminal cluster, individual flowers about ¼" (6 mm) wide, with 5 petals, nodding. **PLANT:** 2–10" (5–25 cm) tall; leaves appearing basal, simple, ovate to nearly round, margin minutely toothed, green. **HABITAT:** woodlands.

One-flowered Pyrola, One-flowered Wintergreen

- *Moneses uniflora* (L.) Gray
- Heath family **Ericaceae**

FLOWERING SEASON: mid-June to early July. **FLOWERS:** white, solitary, terminal, about ¾" (2 cm) wide, with 5 broad petals. **PLANT:** 2–6" (5–15.5 cm) tall; leaves 2–6, opposite or whorled but appearing basal, simple, rounded to ovate, margin with minute rounded teeth, green. **HABITAT:** woodlands.

One-flowered Pyrola / *Moneses uniflora*

Round-leaf Pyrola / *Pyrola americana*

Virgin's-bower / *Clematis virginiana*

Partridge-berry, Twin-berry / *Mitchella repens*

Spathulate-leaved Sundew / *Drosera intermedia*

One-sided Pyrola / *Orthilia secunda*

Early Saxifrage
•*Saxifraga virginiensis* Michx.
•Saxifrage family **Saxifragaceae**
FLOWERING SEASON: late April through May.   FLOWERS: white, many on a branched terminal cluster, up to ¼" (6 mm) wide, with 5 rounded petals. PLANT: 4–12" (10–30 cm) tall; leaves mostly basal, simple, ovate with a bluntly toothed margin, green.   HABITAT: rocky, usually moist soils, often on wet cliffs.

Grass-of-Parnassus
•*Parnassia glauca* Raf.
•Saxifrage family **Saxifragaceae**
FLOWERING SEASON: August-September. FLOWER: white with greenish veins, solitary, terminal, about 1" (2.5 cm) wide, with 5 oval petals.   PLANT: 8–24" (20–60 cm) tall; leaves mostly basal, with 1 on the stem, simple, broadly egg-shaped to nearly round, margin entire, green.   HABITAT: swamps and moist meadows.

Foamflower
•*Tiarella cordifolia* L.
•Saxifrage family **Saxifragaceae**
FLOWERING SEASON: mid-May to mid-June. FLOWERS: white, about a dozen in a narrow terminal cluster, about ¼" (6 mm) wide, with 5 narrow petals and 10 long, conspicuous stamens that give the flower a feathery appearance. PLANT: 6–12" (15–30 cm) tall; leaves basal, simple, heart-shaped with 3 to 7 angular lobes, margins toothed, green.   HABITAT: woodlands.

Diapensia
•*Diapensia lapponica* L.
•Diapensia family **Diapensiaceae**
FLOWERING SEASON: June-July. FLOWERS: white, several to many, each on individual stalks, terminal, about ⅜" (1 cm) wide, with 5 rounded lobes. PLANT: a low shrub forming dense cushion-like tufts, 1–3" (2.5–7.5 cm) tall; leaves in crowded basal rosettes, simple, spathulate, leathery, margin entire, evergreen. HABITAT: mountain summits.

Dewdrop, False Violet
•*Dalibarda repens* L.
•Rose family **Rosaceae**
FLOWERING SEASON: late July to mid-August. FLOWERS: white, 1 or 2 arising in leaf axils, about ⅜" (9 mm) wide, with 5 rounded petals. PLANT: creeping, 2–6" (5–15 cm) long; leaves basal, simple, heart-shaped, margin scalloped, pubescent on both sides, green. HABITAT: open woodlands and fen borders.

LEAVES BASAL, COMPOUND

Goldthread
•*Coptis trifolia* (L.) Salisb.
•Crowfoot family **Ranunculaceae**
FLOWERING SEASON: May.   FLOWER: white, solitary, terminal, about ½" (1.3 cm) wide, with 5 to 7 lance-shaped, petal-like sepals. PLANT: 3–6" (7.5–15 cm) tall; leaves basal, long-stalked, compound with 3 fan-shaped, sharply toothed leaflets, green, glossy, evergreen. HABITAT: damp woods. COMMENTS: named for its slender yellow-orange roots.

Dewdrop, False Violet / *Dalibarda repens*

Goldthread / *Coptis trifolia*

Early Saxifrage / *Saxifraga virginiensis*

Foamflower / *Tiarella cordifolia*

Diapensia / *Diapensia lapponica*

Grass-of-Parnassus / *Parnassia glauca*

Wild Strawberry

- *Fragaria virginiana* Dcne.
- Rose family **Rosaceae**

FLOWERING SEASON: May. FLOWERS: white with a yellow center, few, in a terminal cluster, about ¾" (1.9 cm) wide, with 5 rounded petals. PLANT: creeping, 3–6" (7.5–15 cm) tall; leaves appearing basal, 3-lobed; leaflets broadly oval to obovate, margins toothed, green; fruit red, ovoid, fragrant, edible. HABITAT: fields and edges of woodlands.

Common Wood-sorrel

- *Oxalis acetosella* L.
- Oxalis family **Oxalidaceae**

FLOWERING SEASON: late May through July. FLOWERS: pinkish white to white with dark pink veins, solitary to several in leaf axils, about ¾" (1.9 cm) wide, with 5 rounded petals. PLANT: 2–6" (5–15 cm) tall; leaves appearing basal, compound with 3 leaflets; leaflets heart-shaped, margin entire, green. HABITAT: moist woodlands.

Buckbean, Bogbean

- *Menyanthes trifoliata* L.
- Buckbean family **Menyanthaceae**

FLOWERING SEASON: late May to early June. FLOWERS: white, several to many in a terminal cluster, about ½" (1.3 cm) long, tubular with 5 spreading, hairy, petal-like lobes. PLANT: 4–8" (10–20 cm) tall; leaves basal, with three leaflets; leaflets obovate, margins entire, green. HABITAT: bogs, fens, and along ponds.

LEAVES ALTERNATE, SIMPLE

Poke, Pokeweed

- *Phytolacca americana* L.
- Pokeweed family **Phytolaccaceae**

FLOWERING SEASON: July to early August. FLOWERS: white with a green center, many on slender 2–8" (5–20cm) long, loosely flowered terminal and axial clusters, up to ¼" (6 mm) wide, with 5 rounded, petal-like divisions. PLANT: 4–12' (1.2–3.6 m) tall; leaves alternate on a purplish stem, large, simple, broadly lance-shaped, margin entire, green; fruit a grape-like cluster of very dark purple inedible berries. HABITAT: meadows and woodlots.

Japanese Knotweed, Japanese Bamboo

- *Polygonum cuspidatum* Sieb. and Zucc.
- Buckwheat family **Polygonaceae**

FLOWERING SEASON: mid-August through September. FLOWERS: white, many in slender, 2–4" (5–10 cm) long terminal and upper axial clusters, minute, with 5 petal-like lobes. PLANT: 4–8' (1.2–2.4 m) tall; appearing shrub-like but stems not perennial; leaves alternate on a bamboo-like stem, simple, broadly ovate with a somewhat squared base, margin entire, green. HABITAT: fields, waste areas, roadsides, thickets, and moist soil

Cheese Mallow

- *Malva neglecta* Wallr.
- Mallow family **Malvaceae**

FLOWERING SEASON: June-August. FLOWERS: whitish with lavender veins, sometimes with a bluish tinge, 1 to several, in axils along the stem, about ½" (1.3 cm) wide with 5 broad petals notched at the tip. PLANT: 4–12" (10–30 cm) long, mostly prostrate; leaves alternate, simple, heart-shaped with a rounded tip, shallowly lobed, margin scalloped to somewhat toothed, green. HABITAT: fields and waste areas. COMMENTS: called cheeses in reference to the wheel-shaped fruit.

Cheese Mallow / *Malva neglecta*

Buckbean, Bogbean / *Menyanthes trifoliata*

Poke, Pokeweed / *Phytolacca americana*

Wild Strawberry / *Fragaria virginiana*

Common Wood-sorrel / *Oxalis acetosella*

Japanese Knotweed, Japanese Bamboo / *Polygonum cuspidatum*

Labrador Tea
- *Rhododendron groenlandicum* (Oeder) Kron & Judd
- Heath family **Ericaceae**

FLOWERING SEASON: June. **FLOWERS:** white, several to many in a rounded terminal cluster, ¼–⅜" (6–9 mm) wide, tubular at the base with 5 spreading, petal-like lobes. **PLANT:** shrub, about 1–3' (30–90 cm) tall; leaves alternate, simple, oblong with an inrolled margin, dark green above, downy and white (young leaves) to rusty (mature leaves) below, evergreen. **HABITAT:** bogs, fens, swamps, and drier acidic soils. **COMMENTS:** specimens growing at higher elevations are often stunted.

Great Laurel
- *Rhododendron maximum* L.
- Heath family **Ericaceae**

FLOWERING SEASON: July. **FLOWERS:** white to pale pink, with a sprinkling of gold-green dots on the inner surface, many in large globular terminal clusters, ¾"–1¼" (2–3 cm) wide, tubular at the base with 5 large oval petal-like lobes. **PLANT:** a shrub, 3–15' (1–4.6 m) or more high; leaves alternate, simple, large, oblong to lance-shaped, margin entire and often curled, green, evergreen. **HABITAT:** shaded moist soils, along streams.

Mountain Laurel
- *Kalmia latifolia* L.
- Heath family **Ericaceae**

FLOWERING SEASON: mid-June to mid-July. **FLOWERS:** white to pinkish, many, in a spherical terminal cluster, ¾–1" (1.9–2.5 cm) wide, saucer-shaped with 5 shallowly pointed lobes. **PLANT:** shrub, 5–15' (1.5–4.5 m) tall; leaves alternate, simple, lance-shaped with an entire margin, green, evergreen. **HABITAT:** in sandy or rocky soil in woodlands. **COMMENTS:** bees visiting these flowers are said to

produce *poisonous* honey.

Trailing Arbutus
- *Epigaea repens* L.
- Heath family **Ericaceae**

FLOWERING SEASON: mid-April to mid-May. **FLOWERS:** white to pink, several, in a terminal cluster, about ½" (1.3 cm) wide, tubular at the base with 5 spreading, petal-like lobes; fragrant. **PLANT:** prostrate on the ground; leaves alternate along a hairy woody stem, simple, oval with an entire margin, green, evergreen. **HABITAT:** sandy or rocky woods, especially under evergreens.

Meadow-sweet
- *Spiraea latifolia* (Ait.) Borkh.
- Rose family **Rosaceae**

FLOWERING SEASON: July to mid-August. **FLOWERS:** white with pinkish centers, many in showy upright, 3–5" (7.5–12.5 cm) terminal and axial clusters, about ⁵⁄₁₆" (8 mm) wide, with 5 rounded petals. **PLANT:** shrub, 2–5' (0.6–1.5 m) tall; leaves alternate, simple, oblong, margin coarsely and unevenly toothed, green. **HABITAT:** swamps, meadows, and roadsides.

Red Chokeberry
- *Aronia arbutifolia* (L.) Pers.
- Rose family **Rosaceae**

FLOWERING SEASON: mid-May to mid-June. **FLOWERS:** white, many in rounded terminal clusters, about ½" (1.2 cm) wide, with 5 rounded petals. **PLANT:** shrub, 3–8' (1–2.4 m) tall; leaves alternate, simple, oval to obovate, margin toothed, green; fruit about ¼" (6 mm) long, apple-like, red, with astringent flesh. **HABITAT:** moist thickets and drier sandy soils.

Great Laurel/*Rhododendron maximum*

Red Chokeberry / *Aronia arbutifolia*

Mountain Laurel / *Kalmia latifolia*

Labrador Tea / *Rhododendron groenlandicum*

Meadow-sweet / *Spiraea latifolia*

Trailing Arbutus / *Epigaea repens*

Choke-cherry
• *Prunus virginiana* L.
• Rose family **Rosaceae**
FLOWERING SEASON: May-June. FLOW-ERS: white, many in slender terminal and axial clusters, about ½" (1.3 cm) wide, with 5 rounded petals. PLANT: shrub, 8–30' (2.4–9.2 m) tall; leaves alternate, simple, ovate with a pointed tip, margin finely toothed, green; fruit about ⅜" (1 cm) wide, round, red to purplish red, astringent. HABITAT: thickets, open woods, abandoned fields, and roadsides.

New Jersey Tea
• *Ceanothus americanus* L.
• Buckthorn family **Rhamnaceae**
FLOWERING SEASON: July. FLOWERS: white, many in long-stalked rounded terminal and axial clusters, minute, with 5 tiny petals. PLANT: shrub, 2–4' (0.6–1.2 m) tall; leaves alternate, simple, ovate with a pointed tip, margin toothed, green. HABITAT: woodlands.

Sweet Pepper-bush
• *Clethra alnifolia* L.
• White Alder family **Clethraceae**
FLOWERING SEASON: July-August. FLOW-ERS: white, many, in numerous slender terminal clusters, about ⅜" (9 mm) wide, with 5 rounded petals; spicy fragrance. PLANT: 3–10' (0.9–3 m) tall; leaves alternate on woody branches, simple, obovate, margin sharply toothed, green. HABITAT: swamps and moist woodlands, mostly near the coast.

Black Nightshade
• *Solanum ptycanthum* Dunal
• Nightshade family **Solanaceae**
FLOWERING SEASON: late July to mid-September. FLOWERS: white with a pro-truding yellow center, few to several, in loose clusters, about ⁵⁄₁₆" (8 mm) wide, corolla with 5 spreading and somewhat recurved, sharply pointed, petal-like lobes. PLANT: 1–2½' (0.3–0.8 m) tall; leaves alternate, simple, ovate, margin usually entire, green; fruit a black berry. HABITAT: waste areas.

Horse-nettle
• *Solanum carolinense* L.
• Nightshade family **Solanaceae**
FLOWERING SEASON: late June through August. FLOWERS: white to bluish white with a protruding yellow center, sever-al, in a loose terminal cluster, about 1" (2.5 cm) wide, corolla shaped like a 5-pointed star. PLANT: about 1–3' (30–90 cm) tall; leaves alternate on a spiny stem, simple, ovate with several deeply cleft, sharply pointed lobes, green. HABITAT: roadsides, meadows, cultivated fields, and waste areas.

Jimsonweed
• *Datura stramonium* L.
• Nightshade family **Solanaceae**
FLOWERING SEASON: August-September. FLOWERS: white, sometimes with a pur-plish center, several, scattered through-out the plant in axils, up to 4" (10 cm) long, corolla bell-shaped with 5 flaring sharp lobes. PLANT: 1–5' (0.3–1.5 m) tall; leaves alternate, simple, ovate, mar-gin with several large, sharp-tipped lobes, green. HABITAT: fields, pastures, and waste areas, sometimes close to the ocean.

Black Nightshade / *Solanum ptycanthum*

Sweet Pepper-bush / *Clethra alnifolia*

New Jersey Tea / *Ceanothus americanus*

Jimsonweed / *Datura stramonium*

Horse-nettle / *Solanum carolinense*

Choke-cherry / *Prunus virginiana*

Moth-mullein
• *Verbascum blatteria* L.
• Figwort family **Scrophulariaceae**
FLOWERING SEASON: mid-June through August. FLOWERS: yellow or white, several, in a loose-flowered, slender terminal cluster, about 1" (2.5 cm) wide, tubular at the base with 5 rounded petal-like lobes. PLANT: 2–6' (0.6–1.8 m) tall; leaves basal and alternate, simple, oblong to lance-shaped with a pointed tip, margin toothed, green. HABITAT: fields and waste areas.

LEAVES ALTERNATE, COMPOUND OR DEEPLY DIVIDED

Multiflora Rose
• *Rosa multiflora* Thunb. ex Murr.
• Rose family **Rosaceae**
FLOWERING FEASON: June. FLOWERS: white with a yellow center, many in axial and terminal clusters; about ¾" (2 cm) wide, with 5 rounded petals; slightly fragrant. PLANT: shrub, 5–10' (1.5–3 m) tall; leaves alternate, pinnately compound with 7–9 leaflets; leaflets ovate with a pointed tip, margins toothed, green. HABITAT: old pastures and roadsides.

Red Raspberry
• *Rubus idaeus* L.
• Rose family **Rosaceae**
FLOWERING SEASON: June. FLOWERS: white, several to many, in loose axial and terminal clusters, about ½" (1.3 cm) wide, with 5 rounded petals. PLANT: shrub, about 3–6' (0.9–1.8 m) tall; leaves alternate, pinnately compound with 5 leaflets on the lower stem and 3 on the upper stem; leaflets oblong with a pointed tip, margins coarsely and irregularly toothed, green; fruit berry-like, round, bright red, juicy; stem spiny. HABITAT: edges of woodlands, woodland trails, and disturbed soils. COMMENTS: raspberry

species have pinnately compound leaves, round stems, and berries that easily separate from their stalks. Blackberry species have palmately compound leaves, angular stems, and berries that are tightly fixed to their stalks.

Dewberry
• *Rubus flagellaris* Willd.
• Rose family **Rosaceae**
FLOWERING SEASON: June. FLOWERS: white, several scattered along the plant, about 1" (2.5 cm) wide, with 5 rounded petals. PLANT: prostrate; leaves alternate on a thorned stem, compound with 3 leaflets; leaflets ovate, margins toothed, green. HABITAT: open woodlands. COMMENTS: the name dewberry is commonly applied to any blackberry or raspberry with a prostrate stem.

White Avens
• *Geum canadense* Jacq.
• Rose family **Rosaceae**
FLOWERING SEASON: mid-June to mid-July. FLOWERS: white, several in terminal clusters, about ⅝" (1.6 cm) wide, with 5 rounded petals. PLANT: 1½–2½' (45–75 cm) tall; leaves basal and alternate; basal leaves with 3 lobes or pinnately compound; stem leaves typically with 3 lobes; leaflets broadly ovate or lance-shaped, margins toothed, green; stem hairy. HABITAT: woodlands.

Tall Cinquefoil
• *Potentilla arguta* Pursh
• Rose family **Rosaceae**
FLOWERING SEASON: June-July. FLOWERS: white with a yellow center, few to several in a rounded terminal cluster, about ½" (1.3 cm) wide, with 5 nearly round petals. PLANT: 1–4' (0.3–1.2 m) tall; leaves alternate, pinnately compound with 7 to 11 leaflets; leaflets ovate, margins toothed, green. HABITAT: dry or rocky soil.

White Avens / *Geum canadense*

Tall Cinquefoil / *Potentilla arguta*

Dewberry / *Rubus flagellaris*

Multiflora Rose / *Rosa multiflora*

Red Raspberry / *Rubus idaeus*

Moth-mullein / *Verbascum blatteria*

Three-toothed Cinquefoil

•*Potentilla tridentata* Soland. ex Ait.

•Rose family **Rosaceae**

FLOWERING SEASON: July-August. **FLOW-ERS:** white, 1–6, terminal, about ⁵⁄₁₆" (8 mm) wide, with 5 rounded petals. **PLANT:** 1–12" (2.5–30 cm) tall; leaves alternate, 3-lobed; leaflets oblong to lance-shaped, margins entire except for 2–5 teeth at the tip, green, evergreen. **HABITAT:** rocky or sandy soil, often at higher elevations.

Meadow-sweet, Queen-of-the meadow

•*Filipendula ulmaria* (L.) Maxim.

•Rose family **Rosaceae**

FLOWERING SEASON: mid-to late July. **FLOWERS:** white to off-white, many in a large, showy terminal cluster, about ⅜" (9 mm) wide, with 5 rounded petals; fragrant. **PLANT:** 2–4' (0.6–1.2 m) tall; leaves alternate, pinnately compound; leaflets ovate to lance-shaped, margins toothed, green. **HABITAT:** meadows.

Cow-parsnip

•*Heracleum maximum* Bartr.

•Carrot family **Apiaceae**

FLOWERING SEASON: June. **FLOWERS:** white, many, in rounded, flat-topped terminal clusters 6–12" (15–30 cm) wide; individual flowers tiny, with 5 petals. **PLANT:** 4–8' (1.2–2.4 m) tall; leaves alternate, compound with 3 leaflets; leaflets broadly ovate, often lobed, margins toothed, green, stem green. **HABITAT:** moist, usually shaded, soils.

Poison Hemlock

•*Conium maculatum* L.

•Carrot family **Apiaceae**

FLOWERING SEASON: mid-June to mid-July. **FLOWERS:** white, many in numerous rounded, flat-topped, terminal and axial clusters 1–3" (2.5–7.5 cm) wide; individual flowers tiny, with 5 petals. **PLANT:** 2–5' (0.6–1.5 m) tall; leaves alternate, with 3 large pinnately compound divisions, fern-like; leaflets ovate, margins toothed and deeply divided, green; stem green, usually with purplish markings. **HABITAT:** waste areas, roadsides and moist meadows. **COMMENTS:** *extremely poisonous.*

Water-hemlock, Spotted Cowbane

•*Cicuta maculata* L.

•Carrot family **Apiaceae**

FLOWERING SEASON: July. **FLOWERS:** white, many, in rounded, flat-topped terminal clusters 2–4" (5–10 cm) wide; individual flowers tiny, with 5 petals. **PLANT:** 3–6' (0.9–1.8 m) tall; leaves alternate, pinnately compound; 7 to 17 leaflets, lance-shaped with sharp tips, basal leaflets often deeply cleft, margins coarsely toothed, green; stem green with purplish markings. **HABITAT:** swamps and low grounds. **COMMENTS:** *extremely poisonous.* Water-parsnip, *Sium suave*, has narrowly lance-shaped, finely toothed leaflets.

Bulb-bearing Water-hemlock

•*Cicuta bulbifera* L.

•Carrot family **Apiaceae**

FLOWERING SEASON: July-August. **FLOW-ERS:** white, many, in small, rounded terminal and axial clusters about 1" (2.5 cm) wide; individual flowers with 5 tiny petals. **PLANT:** 1–3½' (0.3–1.1 m) tall; leaves alternate, divided into several pinnately compound sections; leaflets very narrow, margins sharply toothed, green; bulblet clusters in leaf axils. **HABITAT:** swamps, edges of ponds and lakes. **COMMENTS:** *extremely poisonous.*

Poison Hemlock / *Conium maculatum*

Three-toothed Cinquefoil / *Potentilla tridentata*

Bulb-bearing Water-hemlock / *Cicuta bulbifera*

Cow-parsnip / *Heracleum maximum*

Water-hemlock, Spotted Cowbane / *Cicuta maculata*

Meadow-sweet, Queen-of-the-meadow / *Filipendula ulmaria*

Queen-Anne's Lace, Wild Carrot
•*Daucus carota* L.
•Carrot family **Apiaceae**
FLOWERING SEASON: July to mid-September. **FLOWERS:** white, often with a single tiny purple flower in the center of each cluster, many, in rounded, flat-topped terminal clusters 2–4" (5–10 cm) wide; individual flowers tiny, with 5 petals. **PLANT:** about 1–3' (0.3–1 m) tall; leaves alternate, with 1 to 3 deeply cleft, pinnately arranged divisions, fern-like, margins toothed, green. **HABITAT:** fields and waste areas. **COMMENTS:** caraway, *Carum carvi*, also found in sunny areas, is only 1–2' (30–60 cm) tall, has flower clusters 1–2½" (2.5–6.3 cm) wide, and narrower leaves.

Virginia Waterleaf
•*Hydrophyllum virginianum* L.
•Waterleaf family **Hydrophyllaceae**
FLOWERING SEASON: June. **FLOWERS:** white to violet, several, in a small, rounded cluster, about ⁵⁄₁₆" (8 mm) long, tubular with 5 oblong, petal-like lobes. **PLANT:** 1–2' (30–60 cm) tall; leaves alternate, pinnately lobed into 5 to 7 sharply toothed segments, green, often with whitish mottling. **HABITAT:** woodlands. **COMMENTS:** broad-leaved waterleaf, *Hydrophyllum canadense*, has similar flowers but broad, maple-like leaves.

Yarrow
•*Achillea millefolium* L.
•Aster family **Asteraceae**
FLOWERING SEASON: mid-June to early September. **FLOWERS:** white, sometimes pinkish, many in a rounded, flat-topped terminal cluster, about 2" (5 cm) wide, individual flowerheads about ¼" (6 mm) wide, rimmed with 4 to 6 petal-like rays. **PLANT:** 1–2' (30–61 cm) tall; leaves basal and alternate, finely dissected into pinnatified segments, lance-shaped, green.

HABITAT: fields, roadsides, and waste areas.

LEAVES OPPOSITE OR WHORLED, SIMPLE

Carolina Spring Beauty
•*Claytonia caroliniana* Michx.
•Purslane family **Portulacaceae**
FLOWERING SEASON: mid-April to mid-May. **FLOWERS:** white to pinkish with darker pink veins, few, in a loose terminal cluster, about ¾" (1.9 cm) wide, with 5 rounded petals. **PLANT:** 2–4" (5–10 cm) tall; leaves basal or opposite, simple, broadly lance-shaped, margin entire, green. **HABITAT:** woodlands. **COMMENTS:** Spring beauty, *Claytonia virginica*, has much narrower leaves.

Bouncing-bet, Soapwort
•*Saponaria officinalis* L.
•Pink family **Caryophyllaceae**
FLOWERING SEASON: mid-July to early September. **FLOWERS:** white to pinkish white, many in a dense, rounded terminal cluster, about 1" (2.5 cm) wide, with 5 broad, slightly notched petals. **PLANT:** 1–2' (30–60 cm) tall; leaves opposite, simple, ovate with a pointed tip, margin entire, green. **HABITAT:** roadsides, fields, and waste areas.

Mountain Sandwort
•*Arenaria groenlandica* (Retz) Spreng.
•Pink family **Caryophyllaceae**
FLOWERING SEASON: June-September. **FLOWERS:** white, many, terminal; up to ½" (1.2 cm) wide, with 5 rounded petals. **PLANT:** densely tufted, 2–5" (5–12.5 cm) tall; leaves opposite, simple, narrowly lance-shaped, margin entire, green. **HABITAT:** in rocky areas, especially on mountains.

Yarrow / *Achillea millefolium*

Queen-Anne's Lace, Wild Carrot /
Daucus carota

Bouncing-Bet, Soapwort / *Saponaria officinalis*

Mountain Sandwort / *Arenaria groenlandica*

Virginia Waterleaf / *Hydrophyllum virginianum*

Carolina Spring Beauty / *Claytonia caroliniana*

Mouse-ear Chickweed

- *Cerastium fontanum* Baumg. *emend* Jalas.
- Pink family **Caryophyllaceae**

FLOWERING SEASON: May into September. **FLOWERS:** white, several, in loose terminal clusters, about ¼" (6 mm) wide, with 5 petals deeply cleft nearly to the base. **PLANT:** spreading, 4–12" (10–30 cm) tall; leaves opposite and basal, oblong, hairy, margin entire, green. **HABITAT:** fields, meadows, and lawns. **COMMENTS:** common chickweed, *Stellaria media*, has broader, hairless leaves.

White Campion

- *Silene latifolia* Poir.
- Pink family **Caryophyllaceae**

FLOWERING SEASON: June to early August. **FLOWERS:** white to pinkish white, few in a loose terminal cluster, about ¾" (1.9 cm) wide, with 5 notched petals and an inflated, hairy, bladder-like base. **PLANT:** 1–2' (30–60 cm) tall; leaves opposite, simple, broadly lance-shaped, margin entire, green. **HABITAT:** fields and waste areas.

Pipsissewa, Prince's Pine

- *Chimaphila umbellata* (L.) Bart.
- Shinleaf family **Pyrolaceae**

FLOWERING SEASON: mid-to late July. **FLOWERS:** white to pinkish white, few to several in a loose terminal cluster, about ½" (1.3 cm) wide, with 5 rounded petals. **PLANT:** 4–10" (10–25 cm) tall; leaves opposite or whorled, simple, broadly lance-shaped, margin toothed, glossy, green, evergreen. **HABITAT:** woodlands.

Miterwort

- *Mitella diphylla* L.
- Saxifrage family **Saxifragaceae**

FLOWERING SEASON: May. **FLOWERS:** white, many on an erect 6–8" (15–20 cm) tall, wand-like cluster, about ⅛" (3 mm) wide, with 5 feathery petals. **PLANT:** 10–18" (25–45 cm) tall; leaves of 2 types, basal leaves heart-shaped and long-stalked, and a pair of opposite, somewhat lance-shaped leaves about one-third of the way up the stem, margins toothed, green. **HABITAT:** rich woodlands.

Hobblebush

- *Viburnum lantanoides* Michx.
- Honeysuckle family **Caprifoliaceae**

FLOWERING SEASON: late April through May. **FLOWERS:** white, many in showy, 3–5" (7.5–12.5 cm) wide flat-topped axial clusters, flowers of two types; peripheral flowers large, showy, sterile, about 1" (2.5 cm) wide, corolla with 5 rounded petal-like lobes; central flowers small, fertile, corolla with 5 tiny petal-like lobes. **PLANT:** 2–10' (0.6–3.1 m) tall; leaves opposite on woody stems, simple, nearly round, margin toothed, green; fruit purplish black. **HABITAT:** woodlands. **COMMENTS:** highbush cranberry, *Viburnum trilobum*, has similar flower clusters but has 3-lobed maple-like leaves and translucent-appearing red fruit.

Galinsoga, Quickweed

- *Galinsoga ciliata* (Raf.) Blake
- Aster family **Asteraceae**

FLOWERING SEASON: mid-June to October. **FLOWERHEADS:** white with a yellow center, many, several in leaf axils, individual flowerheads about ¼" (6 mm) wide, usually rimmed with five 3-toothed petal-like rays. **PLANT:** 6–19" (15–48 cm) tall; leaves opposite, simple, ovate, margin toothed, green; stems hairy. **HABITAT:** fields and waste places.

Pipsissewa, Prince's Pine / *Chimaphila umbellata*

Hobblebush / *Viburnum lantanoides*

Miterwort / *Mitella diphylla*

Galinsoga, Quickweed / *Galinsoga ciliata*

Mouse-ear Chickweed / *Cerastium fontanum*

White Campion / *Silene latifolia*

LEAVES OPPOSITE OR WHORLED, COMPOUND OR DEEPLY DIVIDED

Canada Anemone, Windflower

•*Anemone canadensis* L.
•Crowfoot family **Ranunculaceae**
FLOWERING SEASON: late May to early July. FLOWERS: white, usually 1 to 3, terminal, about 1¼" (3.1 cm) wide, with 5 large, oblong, petal-like sepals. PLANT: 1–2' (30–60 cm) tall; leaves of 2 types, basal leaves long-stalked and 5-lobed, leaves along upper stem whorled or paired, stalkless and 3-lobed, margins sharply and deeply toothed, green; seedhead rounded. HABITAT: low, moist meadows. COMMENTS: long-headed thimbleweed, *Anemone cylindrica*, has upper leaves with lobes divided to their base and a long, cylindrical seedhead.

Dwarf Ginseng

•*Panax trifolius* L.
•Ginseng family **Araliaceae**
FLOWERING SEASON: early to mid-May. FLOWERS: white, several in a small, circular terminal cluster, about ¹⁄₁₆" (1.6 mm) wide, with 5 petals and 5 prominent stamens. PLANT: 3–8" (7.5–20 cm) tall; leaves 3, whorled about the stem, palmately compound, with 3 to 5 leaflets; leaflets narrowly lance-shaped, margins toothed, green. HABITAT: woodlands.

Blue Elderberry

•*Sambucus canadensis* L.
•Honeysuckle family **Caprifoliaceae**
FLOWERING SEASON: mid-June to mid-July. FLOWERS: white, many in showy, broad, flat-topped clusters, about ³⁄₁₆" (5 mm) wide, corolla with 5 tiny petal-like lobes. PLANT: 4–10' (1.2–3.1 m) tall; leaves opposite on woody stems, pinnately compound with 5 to 7, usually 7, leaflets; leaflets ovate with a pointed tip, margins toothed, green; fruit purple-black, edible. HABITAT: fields and hedgerows. COMMENTS: red elderberry, *Sambucus racemosa*, has cylindrical clusters of dull yellow-white flowers and poisonous red fruit; habitat woodlands.

Garden Valerian

•*Valeriana officinalis* L.
•Valerian family **Valerianaceae**
FLOWERING SEASON: June-July. FLOWERS: pinkish white to off-white, many, in showy rounded terminal clusters, about ⅛" (4 mm) long, tubular with 5 petal-like lobes. PLANT: 2–5' (0.6–1.5 m) tall; leaves opposite, simple, deeply and pinnately divided into 7 to 15 or more narrow lobes, margins sharply toothed, green. HABITAT: fields and roadsides.

FLOWERS SYMMETRICAL, WITH 6 PETALS OR PETAL-LIKE PARTS

LEAVES BASAL, SIMPLE

Wild Leek, Ramp

•*Allium tricoccum* Ait.
•Lily family **Liliaceae**
FLOWERING SEASON: July. FLOWERS: white, many in a nearly spherical terminal cluster on a thin, leafless stalk, about ¼" (6 mm) long, perianth with 6 nonspreading parts that give the flower a somewhat tubular appearance. PLANT: 1–2' (30–60 cm) tall; leaves usually 2, basal, simple, oblong to lance-shaped, emerging early but withering and disappearing well before flowering, green. HABITAT: woodlands. COMMENTS: both the leaves and the bulbs are eagerly sought for their powerful garlic-like flavor.

Canada Anemone, Windflower / *Anemone canadensis*

Blue Elderberry / *Sambucus canadensis*

Dwarf Ginseng / *Panax trifolius*

Garden Valerian / *Valeriana officinalis*

Wild Leek, Ramp / *Allium tricoccum*

Wild Garlic

- *Allium canadense* L.
- Lily family **Liliaceae**

FLOWERING SEASON: June.   **FLOWERS:** white to pinkish-white, 1 to 3 or more in a terminal cluster with usually 3 sheathing papery bracts beneath, about ¼" (6 mm) wide, perianth with 6 widely spreading, lance-shaped, petal-like parts. **PLANT:** about 1' (30 cm) tall; leaves basal or nearly so, very long and narrow, slightly flattened, green. **HABITAT:** fields, moist meadows. **COMMENTS:** field garlic, *Allium vineale*, is a similar naturalized species with hollow leaves and a single papery bract beneath the flower cluster. Individual flowers have a distinct violet to purplish tinge and a nonspreading perianth, giving the flowers a somewhat tubular appearance.

False Asphodel, Sticky Tofieldia

- *Tofieldia glutinosa* (Michx.) Pers.
- Lily family **Liliaceae**

FLOWERING SEASON: mid-June to early July. **FLOWERS:** white, many in an oblong terminal cluster, about ¼" (6 mm) wide, perianth with 6 narrow, petal-like parts. **PLANT:** 6–20" (15–50 cm) tall; leaves 2 to 4, basal, simple, long and narrow, flattened, margin entire, green. **HABITAT:** bogs and along rivers. **COMMENTS:** *endangered. Do not disturb.* The alternate common name sticky tofieldia refers to the adhesive stem.

LEAVES ALTERNATE, SIMPLE

False Solomon's Seal

- *Maianthemum racemosa* L.
- Lily family **Liliaceae**

FLOWERING SEASON: late May to mid-June. **FLOWERS:** white to off-white, many in a branched terminal cluster 1–4" (2.5–10 cm) long, individual flowers about ³⁄₁₆" (5 mm) wide, perianth with 6 oblong petal-like parts. **PLANT:** 1–3'

(30–90 cm) long; leaves alternate, simple, broadly lance-shaped, margin entire, green; fruit a finely speckled pinkish berry. **HABITAT:** woodlands.

Starry False Solomon's Seal

- *Maianthemum stellata* L.
- Lily family **Liliaceae**

FLOWERING SEASON: mid-May to mid-June. **FLOWERS:** white, several in a short but showy terminal cluster, about ½" (1.3 cm) wide; perianth with 6 long, narrow, petal-like parts.   **PLANT:** 8–20" (20–50 cm) tall; leaves alternate, simple, lance-shaped with bases somewhat clasping the stem, margin entire, green; fruit a greenish berry with 6 black stripes. **HABITAT:** moist woodlands, swamps.

Three-leaved Solomon's Seal

- *Maianthemum trifolia* L.
- Lily family **Liliaceae**

FLOWERING SEASON: June.   **FLOWERS:** white, several in a terminal cluster, about ³⁄₈" (9 mm) wide, perianth with 6 lance-shaped, petal-like parts. **PLANT:** 2–15" (5–37.5 cm) tall; leaves usually 3, alternate, simple, lance-shaped with base somewhat clasping the stem, margin entire, green; fruit a red berry. **HABITAT:** bogs, fens, moist woodlands.

White Mandarin

- *Streptopus amplexifolius* (L.) DC.
- Lily family **Liliaceae**

FLOWERING SEASON: June.   **FLOWERS:** greenish white, several, found singly or occasionally two in axils, about ½" (1.3 cm) long, bell-shaped with 6 sharply pointed deeply recurved tips, pendant. **PLANT:** 1½–3' (45–90 cm) tall; leaves alternate along an angularly twisted stalk, simple, broadly lance-shaped with a rounded base that clasps the stem, margin entire, green. **HABITAT:** moist woodlands and wooded swamps.

False Asphodel, Sticky Tofieldia / *Tofieldia glutinosa*

Three-leaved Solomon's Seal / *Maianthemum trifolia*

False Solomon's Seal / *Maianthemum racemosa*

Starry False Solomon's Seal / *Maianthemum stellata*

Wild Garlic / *Allium canadense*

White Mandarin / *Streptopus amplexifolius*

Wild Cucumber, Wild Balsam-apple, Prickly Cucumber

- *Echinocystis lobata* (Michx.) Tour. and Gray
- Gourd family **Cucurbitaceae**

FLOWERING SEASON: August to early September. **FLOWERS:** white, many, in erect, slender axial clusters, about ⅝" (1.6 cm) wide, with 6 very narrow petal-like lobes. **PLANT:** climbing vine, 15–25' (4.5–7.5 m) long; leaves alternate, simple, maple-like with 3 to 7 lobes; margin minutely toothed, green; fruit about 2" (5 cm) long, ovoid, coated with slender flexible spines. **HABITAT:** riverbanks, hedgerows, and waste areas.

LEAVES OPPOSITE, DEEPLY LOBED

May-apple

- *Podophyllum peltatum* L.
- Barberry family **Berberidaceae**

FLOWERING SEASON: mid-May to mid-June. **FLOWERS:** white, solitary, axial, about 2" (5 cm) wide, with usually 6 broad, petal-like sepals and 6 to 9 tiny oblong petals in the center. **PLANT:** 1–1½' (30–45 cm) tall; leaves 2 on flowering plants, opposite, appearing terminal, deeply cleft into 5 to 7 lobes, margin toothed, green. **HABITAT:** woodlands.

FLOWERS SYMMETRICAL, WITH 7 OR MORE PETALS OR PETAL-LIKE PARTS

AQUATIC, LEAVES FLOATING

White Water-lily, Fragrant Water-lily

- *Nymphaea odorata* Dryand. ex Ait.
- Waterlily family **Nymphaeaceae**

FLOWERING SEASON: mid-June to mid-August. **FLOWERS:** white, solitary, terminal, 3–5½" (7.5–13.8 cm) wide, with numerous narrowly oblong petals; fragrant. **PLANT:** leaves up to 1' (30 cm) long, floating, nearly round with a deeply cleft base, margin entire, green on upper surface, purplish below. **HABITAT:** aquatic (ponds, lakes, and slowly moving streams).

LEAVES BASAL, SIMPLE

English Daisy, Lawn Daisy

- *Bellis perennis* L.
- Aster family **Asteraceae**

FLOWERING SEASON: April-May. **FLOWERHEADS:** white to pinkish white with a yellow center, solitary to several, terminal, individual flowerheads ½–1" (1.3–2.5 cm) wide, rimmed with numerous petal-like rays. **PLANT:** 1–8" (2.5–20 cm) tall; leaves basal, simple, obovate, margin slightly toothed, green. **HABITAT:** lawns and waste areas.

LEAVES BASAL, LOBED OR DEEPLY DIVIDED

Bloodroot

- *Sanguinaria canadensis* L.
- Poppy family **Papaveraceae**

FLOWERING SEASON: April. **FLOWERS:** white, solitary, terminal, about 1¼" (3.1 cm) wide, with 8 to 12 oblong petals. **PLANT:** 6–14" (15–35 cm) tall; leaves basal, palmate, with 5 to 9 lobes, margin uneven, green. **HABITAT:** woodlands. **COMMENTS:** the damaged root exudes reddish sap.

Hepatica

- *Hepatica nobilis* Mill.
- Crowfoot family **Ranunculaceae**

FLOWERING SEASON: April-May. **FLOWERS:** pinkish, white or pale blue, several, on individual hairy basal stalks, about ¾" (1.9 cm) wide, with 6 to 12 lance-shaped, petal-like sepals. **PLANT:** 4–6" (10–15 cm) tall; leaves basal with long hairy stalks, simple, 3-lobed, usually with an entire margin, green mottled with purple, evergreen. **HABITAT:** woodlands.

May-apple / *Podophyllum peltatum*

Wild Cucumber, Wild Balsam-apple,
Prickly Cucumber / *Echinocystis lobata*

Bloodroot / *Sanguinaria canadensis*

White Water-lily, Fragrant Water-lily /
Nymphaea odorata

English Daisy, Lawn Daisy / *Bellis perennis*

Hepatica / *Hepatica nobilis*

COMMENTS: both sharp-lobed and blunt-lobed varieties occur in New York.

Twin-leaf

•*Jeffersonia diphylla* (L.) Pers.
•Barberry family **Berberidaceae**
FLOWERING SEASON: mid-April to mid-May. FLOWERS: white, solitary, terminal, about 1" (2.5 cm) wide, with 8 oblong petals. PLANT: 6–8" (15–20 cm) tall when in flower; leaves basal, long-stalked, deeply divided into 2 ovate parts, margin slightly uneven, green. HABITAT: woodlands.

LEAVES ALTERNATE, SIMPLE

Ox-eye Daisy

•*Leucanthemum vulgare* Lam.
•Aster family **Asteraceae**
FLOWERING SEASON: late May to late July. FLOWERHEADS: white with a yellow disc-shaped center; few or solitary, terminal, individual flowerheads 1–2" (2.5–5 cm) wide, rimmed with 20 to 30 narrow, slightly 2–3 toothed, petal-like rays. PLANT: 1–3' (30–90 cm) tall; leaves alternate, simple, somewhat oblong, margins coarsely and unevenly toothed, green. HABITAT: fields and meadows.

Tall White Aster

•*Aster lanceolatus* Willd.
•Aster family **Asteraceae**
FLOWERING SEASON: September. FLOWERHEADS: white with a yellow center, many, terminal and upper axial, about ¾" (1.9 cm) wide, rimmed with about 20 petal-like rays. PLANT: 2–8' (0.6–2.4 m) tall; leaves alternate, simple, lance-shaped, margin toothed, green. HABITAT: moist soil.

Flat-topped White Aster

•*Aster umbellatus* Mill.
•Aster family **Asteraceae**
FLOWERING SEASON: August-September.
FLOWERHEADS: white with a yellow cen-ter, many in a terminal flat-topped cluster, individual flowerheads about ¾" (1.9 cm) wide, rimmed with 10 to 15 petal-like rays. PLANT: 2–8' (0.6–2.4 m) tall; leaves alternate, simple, lance-shaped, margin entire, green. HABITAT: moist soil.

Boott's Rattlesnake-root

•*Prenanthes boottii* (DC.) A. Gray
•Aster family **Asteraceae**
FLOWERING SEASON: July-August. FLOWERHEADS: white, several to many in a terminal cluster, individual flowerheads about ⅜" (1 cm) wide, rimmed by about 10 minutely toothed, narrow, petal-like rays. PLANT: 4–12" (10–30 cm) tall; leaves alternate, simple, of 2 types; basal and lower leaves ovate to arrowhead-shaped, long-stalked; upper leaves ovate to oblong, short-stalked or stalkless; margin entire or finely toothed, green. HABITAT: alpine summits.

LEAVES ALTERNATE, DEEPLY DIVIDED OR LOBED

Mayweed, Stinkweed, Dog-fennel

•*Anthemis cotula* L.
•Aster family **Asteraceae**
FLOWERING SEASON: July into September. FLOWERHEADS: white with a yellow center, several to many in the upper leaf axils, individual flowerheads about 1" (2.5 cm) wide, rimmed with 10 to 18 minutely 3-toothed, petal-like rays. PLANT: 1–2' (30–61 cm) tall; leaves alternate, simple, deeply cleft into numerous narrow pinnately arranged lobes, green, unpleasantly fragrant if torn. HABITAT: fields, roadsides, and waste areas.

Boott's Rattlesnake-root / *Prenanthes boottii*

Ox-eye Daisy / *Leucanthemum vulgare*

Tall White Aster / *Aster lanceolatus*

Twin-leaf / *Jeffersonia diphylla*

Flat-topped White Aster / *Aster umbellatus*

Mayweed, Stinkweed, Dog-fennel / *Anthemis cotula*

LEAVES WHORLED, SIMPLE

Starflower

- *Trientalis borealis* Raf.
- Primrose family **Primulaceae**

FLOWERING SEASON: mid-May to late June. **FLOWERS:** white, 1 to 4, terminal, up to ½" (1.3 cm) wide, with usually 7 petal-like lobes. **PLANT:** 3–9" (7.5–22.5 cm) tall; leaves in a single whorled cluster, simple, lance-shaped, margin minutely toothed, green. **HABITAT:** woodlands.

LEAVES WHORLED AND BASAL, COMPOUND

Rue Anemone

- *Thalictrum thalictrioides* (L.) Eames & Boivin
- Crowfoot family **Ranunculaceae**

FLOWERING SEASON: late April to mid-May. **FLOWERS:** white or occasionally pinkish, 3 or more, terminal, about ¾" (2 cm) wide, with 5" to 10" oval petal-like sepals. **PLANT:** 4–9" (10–22.5 cm) tall; leaves both basal and whorled below flowers, compound; leaflets long-stalked and shallowly 3-lobed, green. **HABITAT:** woodlands.

FLOWERS NOT RADIALLY SYMMETRICAL; MINUTE, FILAMENTOUS, TUBULAR OR APPEARING SO WITH NO PETAL-LIKE LOBES, OR WITH NO OBVIOUS PETAL-LIKE PARTS

LEAVES LACKING

Indian Pipe

- *Monotropa uniflora* L.
- Indian-pipe family **Monotropaceae**

FLOWERING SEASON: July-August. **FLOWERS:** white to pinkish, solitary, terminal, about ¾" (1.9 cm) long, urn-shaped, with 4–6 petals, nodding. **PLANT:** 4–10" (10–25 cm) tall; leaves absent; stalk with numerous, tiny leaf-like bracts, white to pinkish, darkening in age. **HABITAT:** woodlands. **COMMENTS:** although the urn-shaped flowers appear tubular at first glance, close examination reveals symmetrical floral parts.

LEAVES BASAL, SIMPLE

Sweet White Violet

- *Viola macloskeyi* Lloyd
- Violet family **Violaceae**

FLOWERING SEASON: April-May. **FLOWERS:** white, sometimes with fine purple veining, several, on individual stalks; up to ½" (1.3 cm) wide, with 5 unequal, rounded petals. **PLANT:** 1–6" (2.5–15 cm) tall; leaves basal, simple, ovate to nearly round with a heart-shaped base, margin finely toothed, green. **HABITAT:** moist woodlands.

Narrow-leaf Plantain, English Plantain

- *Plantago lanceolata* L.
- Plantain family **Plantaginaceae**

FLOWERING SEASON: late May into July. **FLOWERS:** white, many in a short, ovoid terminal cluster; minute with prominent white-tipped stamens. **PLANT:** 8–20" (20–50 cm) tall; leaves basal, simple, narrowly lance-shaped, margin entire, green. **HABITAT:** fields, lawns, and waste areas. **COMMENTS:** common plantain, *Plantago major*, has broadly ovate leaves and 2–10" (5–25 cm) long, very slender flower clusters.

Narrow-leaf Plantain, English Plantain /
Plantago lanceolata

Rue Anemone / *Thalictrum thalictrioides*

Indian Pipe / *Monotropa uniflora*

Starflower / *Trientalis borealis*

Sweet White Violet / *Viola macloskeyi*

Pussy's-toes
- *Antennaria neglecta* Green
- Aster family **Asteraceae**

FLOWERING SEASON: May. **FLOWER-HEADS:** white, flowerheads several in a cluster in the upper leaf axils, individual flowerheads about ¼" (6 mm) wide. **PLANT:** up to 1' (30 cm) tall; leaves alternate and basal, simple, oblanceolate to narrowly lance-shaped, white, tomentose on the underside, basal leaves with 1 prominent vein, margin entire, green. **HABITAT:** fields and roadsides. **COMMENTS** : everlasting, *Antennaria plantaginifolia*, has broader basal leaves with 3 prominent veins.

Wild Calla
- *Calla palustris* L.
- Arum family **Araceae**

FLOWERING SEASON: mid-May to early June. **FLOWERS:** greenish white, minute, many on a 1" (2.5 cm) long cylindrical spike framed by a 1–2½" (2.5–6.3 cm) long, broadly lance-shaped, pure white, petal-like spathe. **PLANT:** 5–10" (12.5–25 cm) tall; leaves basal, simple, broadly heart-shaped with long stalks, margin entire, green. **HABITAT:** wooded swamps and moist meadows, often in standing water.

Menzies' Rattlesnake Plantain
- *Goodyera oblongifolia* Rafinesque
- Orchid family **Orchidaceae**

FLOWERING SEASON: August. **FLOWERS:** white, often with greenish tinges, 12–24 or more in a densely flowered terminal cluster, about ⅜" (9 mm) long, appearing somewhat pear-shaped, with 6 petal-like parts. **PLANT:** 8–15" (20–38 cm) tall; leaves basal, simple, oblong to egg-shaped, margin entire, dark green to pale bluish green, usually with a conspicuous white stripe along the central vein and white reticulation. **HABITAT:** woodlands.

COMMENTS: *endangered. Do not disturb.* Within the area covered by this book, found only in northernmost Maine.

Slender Ladies' Tresses
- *Spiranthes lacera* (Raf.) Raf.
- Orchid family **Orchidaceae**

FLOWERING SEASON: mid-July to late August **FLOWERS:** white with a greenish center, 5–20 or more loosely spiraled on a slender terminal cluster, about ¼" (5 mm) long, appearing somewhat tubular, with 6 petal-like parts. **PLANT:** 8–24" (20–61 cm) tall; leaves basal, simple, obovate, margin entire, green, may or may not be present during flowering. **HABITAT:** open sandy and often previously disturbed soil.

Small Round-leaved Orchis
- *Amerorchis rotundifolia* (Banks ex Pursh) Hultén
- Orchid family **Orchidaceae**

FLOWERING SEASON: mid-June to early July. **FLOWERS:** white to pinkish white with pinkish purple spots, several on a terminal spike, about ¹¹⁄₁₆" (17 mm) wide, with 5 rounded petal-like parts and a large deeply-lobed lip with a slender basal spur. **PLANT:** 6–10" (15–25 cm) tall; leaf solitary, basal, simple, nearly circular to oval, margin entire, green. **HABITAT:** damp woods and cedar swamps. **COMMENTS:** *endangered. Do not disturb.* Historical in Vermont. Within the area covered by this book, now found only in remote areas of northern and western Maine.

Menzies' Rattlesnake Plantain / *Goodyera oblongifolia*

Wild Calla / *Calla palustris*

Pussy's-toes / *Antennaria neglecta*

Slender Ladies' Tresses / *Spiranthes lacera*

Small Round-leaved Orchis / *Amerorchis rotundifolia*

Large Round-leaved Orchid Complex

• *Platanthera macrophylla* (Goldie) P.M. Brown
• *Platanthera orbiculata* (Pursh) Lindley
• Orchid family **Orchidaceae**

FLOWERING SEASON: late June to mid-August. **FLOWERS**: off-white to greenish white, several to many on a terminal cluster, individual flowers about ¾"–1" (2–2.5 cm) tall, with 6 petal-like parts including a pendant lip; lip of *Platanthera macrophylla* with a 1¹⁄₁₀"–1¾" (2.8–4.6 cm) spur; lip of *Platanthera orbiculata* with a ½–1¹⁄₁₀" (1.4–2.8 cm) spur. **PLANT**: 10–24" (25–60 cm) tall; leaves 2, basal, simple, nearly round, prostrate, margin entire, green, glossy. **HABITAT**: woodlands. **COMMENTS**: some consider these to be a single highly variable species. Reddoch and Reddoch have determined spur length to be the most accurate characteristic for species determination. The only other similar orchid is Hooker's Orchid, *Platanthera hookeri*, which has bright green flowers with an upturned lip.

LEAVES BASAL, COMPOUND OR DEEPLY LOBED

White Clover

• *Trifolium repens* L.
• Bean family **Fabaceae**

FLOWERING SEASON: June–September. **FLOWERS**: off-white, sometimes with a pale pinkish tinge, many, in ¾" (1.9 cm) tall ovoid flowerheads; individual flowers about ¼" (6 mm) long, narrow. **PLANT**: trailing, 4–12" (10–30 cm) long; leaves alternate but appearing basal, compound with 3 leaflets; leaflets obovate, margins finely toothed, green with a pale green chevron. **HABITAT**: fields, lawns, and waste areas.

Squirrel-corn

• *Dicentra canadensis* (Goldie) Walp.
• Fumitory family **Fumariaceae**

FLOWERING SEASON: late April to mid-May. **FLOWERS**: white to greenish white with a pinkish tint, 4 to 8 in a slender terminal cluster, up to ¾" (1.9 cm) long, heart-shaped and open near the tip, nodding. **PLANT**: 6–12" (15–30 cm) tall; leaves basal, compound with many long, narrow divisions, green. **HABITAT**: woodlands.

Squirrel-corn / *Dicentra canadensis*

Platanthera macrophylla

Platanthera orbiculata

Platanthera macrophylla

White Clover / *Trifolium repens*

Platanthera orbiculata

Dutchman's-breeches

• *Dicentra cucullaria* (L.) Bernh.
• Fumitory family **Fumariaceae**
FLOWERING SEASON: mid-April to mid-May.   FLOWERS: white, golden yellow near the tip, several in a slender terminal cluster, about ¾" (1.9 cm) long, V-shaped and open near the tip, nodding. PLANT: 5–10" (12.5–25 cm) tall; leaves basal, compound with many long, narrow divisions, green. HABITAT: woodlands.

LEAVES ALTERNATE, SIMPLE

Golden-seal

• *Hydrastis canadensis* L.
• Crowfoot family **Ranunculaceae**
FLOWERING SEASON: May.   FLOWER: greenish white, solitary, terminal, about ⅜" (9 mm) wide, composed of a rounded cluster of thread-like stamens. PLANT: about 1' (30 cm) tall; leaves 3, 1 basal and 2 alternate on the stem, maple-like with 5 to 9 lobes, margin sharply and unequally toothed, green. HABITAT: woodlands. COMMENTS: *endangered. Do not disturb.*

Canada Violet

• *Viola canadensis* L.
• Violet family **Violaceae**
FLOWERING SEASON: May-June.   FLOWERS: pale violet to nearly white with a yellow center surrounded by fine purple veining, outer surface purple-tinged, several on individual stalks; about ¾" (1.9 cm) wide, with 5 unequal, rounded petals. PLANT: 3–14" (7.5–35 cm) tall; leaves basal and alternate, simple, somewhat heart-shaped, margin toothed, green. HABITAT: woodlands.

Lowbush Blueberry

• *Vaccinium angustifolium* Ait.
• Heath family **Ericaceae**
FLOWERING SEASON: May.   FLOWERS: white, few to several in loose terminal clusters, about ³⁄₁₆" (5 mm) long, waxy, tubular and bell-shaped with 5 small teeth.   PLANT: shrub, 6–20" (15.5–51 cm) tall, often nearly prostrate; leaves alternate, simple, lance-shaped with a minutely toothed margin, green. HABITAT: dry, rocky, or sandy soil. COMMENTS: produces a delicious fruit.

Velvet-leaf Blueberry

• *Vaccinium myrtilloides* Michx.
• Heath family **Ericaceae**
FLOWERING SEASON: June.   FLOWERS: white, many, in small terminal clusters, nearly ¼" (6 mm) long, waxy, tubular with 5 tiny teeth, nodding.   PLANT: shrub, 6–24" (15–60 cm) tall; leaves alternate, simple, oblong with a pointed tip, margin entire, lower surface pubescent, green. HABITAT: moist soils such as fens and swamps.

Bearberry, Kinnikinic

• *Arctostaphylos uva-ursi* Spreng.
• Heath family **Ericaceae**
FLOWERING SEASON: May-June. FLOWERS: white to pale pink, few in terminal clusters, about ¼" (5 mm) long, tubular with 5 tiny teeth. PLANT: a trailing or spreading shrub, 6–24" (15–60 cm) long; leaves alternate, simple, oblong to oval, leathery, margin entire, evergreen; fruit a red, mealy, edible berry. HABITAT: dry, sandy, or rocky soil.

Dutchman's-breeches / *Dicentra cucullaria*

Golden-seal / *Hydrastis canadensis*

Canada Violet / *Viola canadensis*

Velvet-leaf Blueberry / *Vaccinium myrtilloides*

Lowbush Blueberry / *Vaccinium angustifolium*

Bearberry, Kinnikinic / *Arctostaphylos uva-ursi*

Great Bilberry, Bog Bilberry

• *Vaccinium uliginosum* L.
• Heath family Ericaceae

FLOWERING SEASON: June-July. FLOWERS: white to pink, in small clusters or sometimes solitary, about ¼" (6 mm) long, tubular with 4 or sometimes 5 tiny teeth, nodding. PLANT: a branching shrub, 6–24" (15–60 cm) tall; leaves alternate, simple, obovate to oval, somewhat leathery, margin entire, green; fruit a blue to black berry. HABITAT: summits of mountains.

Wintergreen

• *Gaultheria procumbens* L.
• Heath family Ericaceae

FLOWERING SEASON: July to early August. FLOWERS: white, usually 1 to 3, about ¼" (6 mm) long, urn-shaped, somewhat constricted near the tip with 5 slightly flaring teeth, nodding. PLANT: 2–6" (5–15 cm) tall; leaves alternate, clustered near the top of a woody stem, simple, oval with an obscurely toothed margin, green, glossy, evergreen. HABITAT: woodlands, especially under evergreens. COMMENTS: leaves, pleasantly aromatic when torn, are often used to make a delicious solar tea. The fruit, a bright red berry, is also edible.

Bog Rosemary

• *Andromeda glaucophylla* Link
• Heath family Ericaceae

FLOWERING SEASON: mid-May to mid-June. FLOWERS: white or pinkish, 3 to 8 in a drooping terminal cluster; ¼" (6 mm) long, urn-shaped, constricted near the tip, with 5 slightly flaring teeth, waxy. PLANT: shrub, 3–18" (7.5–45 cm) tall; leaves alternate, simple, narrowly lance-shaped with an entire margin, dark green above, downy and white below, evergreen. HABITAT: bogs and fens. COMMENTS: *reportedly poisonous and not to be confused with culinary rose-mary, a member of the mint family.*

Cassandra, Leatherleaf

• *Chamaedaphne calyculata* (L.) Moench
• Heath family Ericaceae

FLOWERING SEASON: mid-April to mid-May. FLOWERS: white, several to many in an extended, 1-sided terminal cluster; about ¼" (6 mm) long, tubular with 5 minute teeth, nodding. PLANT: shrub, 2–4' (0.6–1.2 m) tall; leaves alternate, simple, lance-shaped with an obscurely toothed margin, green, evergreen. HABITAT: bogs, fens and swamps. COMMENTS: the alternate common name leatherleaf refers to the texture of the leaves.

Seneca Snakeroot

• *Polygala senega* L.
• Milkweed family Polygalaceae

FLOWERING SEASON: mid-May through June. FLOWERS: white or tinged green, many in a slender 1–2" (2.5–5 cm) long, terminal cluster; individual flowers about ⅛" (3 mm) long, rounded. PLANT: 6–12" (15–30 cm) tall; leaves alternate, simple, lance-shaped, margin minutely toothed, green. HABITAT: open woodlands.

Field Bindweed

• *Convolvulus arvensis* L.
• Morning Glory family Convolvulaceae

FLOWERING SEASON: late June through July. FLOWERS: white to pale pink, many, scattered 1 to 4 in axial clusters; about 1" (2.5 cm) long and wide, corolla trumpet-shaped. PLANT: trailing, 1–2½' (30–75 cm) long; leaves alternate, simple, arrowhead-shaped, margin entire, green. HABITAT: fields, meadows, and waste areas. COMMENTS: often forms dense mats on the ground.

Cassandra, Leatherleaf / *Chamaedaphne calyculata*

Wintergreen / *Gaultheria procumbens*

Field Bindweed / *Convolvulus arvensis*

Bog Rosemary / *Andromeda glaucophylla*

Great Bilberry, Bog Bilberry / *Vaccinium uliginosum*

Seneca Snakeroot / *Polygala senega*

Hedge Bindweed

- *Calystegia sepium* (L.) R. Br.
- Morning-Glory family **Convolvulaceae**

FLOWERING SEASON: late June through August. FLOWERS: pinkish with 5 white stripes or white throughout, several, axial, individual flowers axial, about 2" (5 cm) long and wide, corolla trumpet-shaped. PLANT: trailing and vine-like, 3–10' (0.9–3 m) long; leaves alternate, simple, triangular, margin entire, green. HABITAT: fields and thickets.

Biennial Gaura

- *Gaura biennis* L.
- Evening Primrose family **Onagraceae**

FLOWERING SEASON: July–August. FLOWERS: white turning pink just before wilting, few to several in small terminal clusters, nearly ½" (1.3 cm) wide, with 4 paddle-shaped petals, all on the upper half of the flower, and 8 conspicuous drooping stamens. PLANT: 2–5' (0.6–1.5 m) tall; leaves alternate, simple, lance-shaped, margin shallowly toothed, green. HABITAT: in dry, sunny soils such as roadsides and fields.

Silverrod, White Goldenrod

- *Solidago bicolor*
- Aster family **Asteraceae**

FLOWERING SEASON: September into October. FLOWERHEADS: white, many in a 2–7" (5–17.5 cm) tall slender terminal or shorter upper axial clusters, individual flowers up to ¼" (6 mm) wide, rimmed with usually 6 or 7 tiny petal-like rays. PLANT: 6–48" (15–120 cm) tall; leaves alternate, simple, obovate to oblong, pubescent, margin finely toothed, green. HABITAT: meadows, roadsides, and woodland borders.

Pearly Everlasting

- *Anaphalis margaritacea* (L.) Benth. and Hook. f. ex Clarke
- Aster family **Asteraceae**

FLOWERING SEASON: August. FLOWERHEADS: white with a yellow center, many, in dense 2–8" (5–20 cm) wide terminal and upper axial clusters, individual flowers about ¼" (6 mm) wide, filamentous, surrounded by numerous pearly, petal-like bracts. PLANT: 1–3' (30–90 cm) tall; leaves alternate, simple, narrowly lance-shaped, pubescent above, woolly below, margin entire, pale green. HABITAT: fields, roadsides, woodland clearings, and waste areas.

Large Solomon's Seal

- *Polygonatum commutatum* (Schultes & Schultes) Dietr.
- Lily family **Liliaceae**

FLOWERING SEASON: late May to early June. FLOWERS: white with greenish tips, many, in axial clusters of 1 to 8, about ¾" (1.9 cm) long, tubularly bell-shaped with 6 small spreading tips, pendant. PLANT: 1–8' (0.3–2.4 m) long; leaves alternate, simple, broadly lance-shaped, margin entire, green. HABITAT: moist woodlands. COMMENTS: the common name Solomon's seal refers to circular stem scars found on the large root.

Ram's Head Lady's Slipper

- *Cypripedium arietinum* R. Br.
- Orchid family **Orchidaceae**

FLOWERING SEASON: mid- to late May. FLOWERS: lip white with reddish purple streaking on the lower surface and sides, sepals and petals purplish brown; usually solitary, terminal; lip about ¾" (2 cm) long, pouch-like with a curious spur-like growth on the lower surface. PLANT: 8–12 (20–30 cm) tall; leaves 3–4, alternate, simple, lance-shaped, margin entire, green. HABITAT: damp woods and lakeshores. COMMENTS: *endangered. Do not disturb.*

Hedge Bindweed / *Calystegia sepium*

Pearly Everlasting / *Anaphalis margaritacea*

Biennial Gaura / *Gaura biennis*

Silverrod, White Goldenrod / *Solidago bicolor*

Large Solomon's Seal / *Polygonatum commutatum*

Ram's Head Lady's Slipper / *Cypripedium arietinum*

Lady's Slipper of the Queen
• *Cypripedium reginae* Walt.
• Orchid family **Orchidaceae**
FLOWERING SEASON: mid-June to the third week of July. **FLOWERS:** lip white with pinkish rose markings, sepals and petals white; 1 or 2, terminal; lip about 1 ¾" (4.5 cm) long, pouch-like. **PLANT:** 12–30" (30–75 cm) tall; leaves 3 to 7, alternate, simple, broadly ovate, margin entire, green. **HABITAT:** fens, swamps, moist meadows, and woods. **COMMENTS:** the tallest lady's slippers found in this region.

White Fringed Orchid
• *Platanthera blephariglottis* (Willd.) Lindl.
• Orchid family **Orchidaceae**
FLOWERING SEASON: mid-July through August. **FLOWERS:** white, 10 to 20 or more, in a dense terminal cluster, about ⅜–⅝" (9 mm–1.5 cm) long, with 5 small, petal-like parts and a large, single-lobed, heavily fringed lip with a slender basal spur. **PLANT:** 12–24" (30–60 cm) tall; leaves alternate, simple, narrowly lance-shaped, margin entire, green. **HABITAT:** sphagnum fens and other open moist areas. **COMMENTS:** ragged fringed orchid, *Platanthera lacera*, has greenish white flowers with a 3-lobed, very deeply fringed lip.

Prairie White Fringed Orchid
• *Platanthera leucophaea* (Nuttall) Lindl.
• Orchid family **Orchidaceae**
FLOWERING SEASON: mid-July to mid-August. **FLOWERS:** creamy white, several to many in a loosely flowered terminal spike; about 1" (2.5 cm) tall and almost as wide, with 5 rounded petal-like parts and a deeply fringed 3-lobed lip with a long slender basal spur. **PLANT:** 1½'–2½' (46–76 cm) tall; leaves alternate, simple, lance-shaped, margin entire, green. **HABITAT:** open moist meadows. **COMMENTS:** *endangered. Do not disturb.* Within the area covered by this book, found only in Aroostook County in north-central Maine.

Tall White Bog Orchid, Bog Candle
• *Platanthera dilatata* (Pursh) Lindl. ex Beck
• Orchid family **Orchidaceae**
FLOWERING SEASON: mid-June through July. **FLOWERS:** white, up to 100 in a dense, slender terminal cluster, about ⅖–⁷⁄₁₀" (10–18 mm) wide, with 6 spreading, petal-like parts, including a lip with a slender basal spur; pleasantly fragrant. **PLANT:** 12–24" (30–60 cm) or more tall; leaves alternate, simple, narrowly lance-shaped, margin entire, green. **HABITAT:** fens and moist meadows.

LEAVES ALTERNATE, COMPOUND OR DEEPLY DIVIDED

Red Baneberry
• *Actaea spicata* L. ssp. *rubra* (Ait.) Hulten
• Crowfoot family **Ranunculaceae**
FLOWERING SEASON: mid- to late May. **FLOWERS:** white, many in a showy rounded terminal cluster about 1¼" (3.1 cm) wide, individual flowers about ¼" (6 mm) wide with many thread-like stamens and 4 to 10 narrow, inconspicuous petals. **PLANT:** 1–2' (30–60 cm) tall; leaves alternate, compound with 9 to 15 leaflets; leaflets variable, margins sharply and unevenly toothed, green; fruit a cylindrical cluster of oval red berries. **HABITAT:** woodlands. **COMMENTS:** white baneberry, *Actaea pachypoda*, also known as doll's eyes, has oval white berries with a prominent black terminal spot.

Tall White Bog Orchid, Bog Candle / *Platanthera dilatata*

Prairie White Fringed Orchid / *Platanthera leucophaea*

Lady's Slipper of the Queen / *Cypripedium reginae*

White Fringed Orchid / *Platanthera blephariglottis*

Red Baneberry / *Actaea spicata* ssp. *rubra*

Tall Meadow-rue

- *Thalictrum pubescens* Pursh
- Crowfoot family **Ranunculaceae**

FLOWERING SEASON: mid-June through July. FLOWERS: white, many, in showy terminal clusters, about ⁵⁄₁₆" (8 mm) wide, composed of a rounded fluffy mass of thread-like stamens. PLANT: about 3–10' (1–3 m) tall; leaves alternate, compound with numerous leaflets; leaflets somewhat oblong with up to 3 shallow lobes, margin entire, green. HABITAT: open, sunny swamps.

Black Snakeroot

- *Cimicifuga racemosa* (L.) Nutt.
- Crowfoot family **Ranunculaceae**

FLOWERING SEASON: July. FLOWERS: white, many, in showy slender terminal clusters up to 2 feet long, about ½" (1.3 cm) wide, composed of rounded clusters of thread-like stamens and 4 to 8 inconspicuous petals; disagreeable fragrance. PLANT: about 3–8' (1–2.4 m) tall; leaves alternate, compound with numerous leaflets; leaflets variable, margins sharply and unevenly toothed, green. HABITAT: woodlands.

Canadian Burnet

- *Sanguisorba canadensis* L.
- Rose family **Rosaceae**

FLOWERING SEASON: August-September. FLOWERS: white, many, in slender 1–6" (2.5–15 cm) cylindrical terminal clusters; about ¼" (6 mm) wide, with 4 prominent filamentous stamens over 4 inconspicuous petal-like parts. PLANT: 1–6' (0.3–1.8 m) tall; leaves alternate, pinnately compound with 7 to 15 leaflets; leaflets narrowly ovate, margins toothed, green. HABITAT: swamps and moist meadows

White Sweet-clover

- *Melilotus alba* Desr. Ex Lam.
- Bean family **Fabaceae**

FLOWERING SEASON: June-August. FLOWERS: white, many, in slender 2–4" (5–10 cm) long, often 1-sided axial clusters, about ¼" (6 mm) long, narrowly pea-like. PLANT: 3–9' (1–2.7 m) tall; leaves alternate, compound with 3 leaflets; leaflets narrowly oblong, margin toothed, green. HABITAT: fields, roadsides, and waste areas.

LEAVES OPPOSITE OR WHORLED, SIMPLE

Enchanter's Nightshade

- *Circaea lutetiana* L.
- Evening Primrose family **Onagraceae**

FLOWERING SEASON: July-August. FLOWERS: white, several, in slender terminal clusters, about ³⁄₁₆" (5 mm) wide, with 2 rounded, notched petals. PLANT: 1–2' (30–60 cm) tall; leaves opposite, simple, ovate, margin shallowly toothed, green. HABITAT: woodlands and waste areas. COMMENTS: small enchanter's nightshade, *Circaea alpina*, is nearly identical but is smaller, up to 8" (20 cm) tall, and has somewhat more coarsely toothed leaves.

Bugleweed

- *Lycopus virginicus* L.
- Mint family **Lamiaceae**

FLOWERING SEASON: late July to mid September. FLOWERS: white, several to many in axillary clusters, tiny, tubular, 4-lobed. PLANT: 6–24" (15–61 cm) tall; leaves opposite on a square stem, simple, oblong to lance-shaped with a pointed tip, margin sharply toothed, green. HABITAT: on wet soil, often near water.

Enchanter's Nightshade / *Circaea lutetiana*

Bugleweed / *Lycopus virginicus*

White Sweet-clover / *Melilotus alba*

Tall Meadow-rue / *Thalictrum pubescens*

Black Snakeroot / *Cimicifuga racemosa*

Canadian Burnet / *Sanguisorba canadensis*

Cow-wheat
•*Melampyrum lineare* Desr.
•Figwort family **Scrophulariaceae**
FLOWERING SEASON: late June into August. FLOWERS: white with a yellow lower lip, several, found in pairs in axils, up to ½" (1.3 cm) long, tubular with 2 short lips. PLANT: 6–18" (15–45 cm) tall; leaves opposite, simple, narrowly lance-shaped, margin entire or with 2 or 3 pairs of sharply pointed teeth near the base, green. HABITAT: woodlands and thickets.

Turtle-heads
•*Chelone glabra* L.
•Figwort family **Scrophulariaceae**
FLOWERING SEASON: late July to early September. FLOWERS: white to faintly pink, several in a terminal cluster; about 1" (2.5 cm) long, tubular and 2-lipped; upper lip large and hood-shaped; lower lip 3-lobed. PLANT: about 1–3' (30–90 cm) tall; leaves opposite, simple, lance-shaped, margin toothed, green. HABITAT: swamps, fens, and along streams.

Thyme Leaf Speedwell
•*Veronica serpyllifolia* L.
•Figwort family **Scrophulariaceae**
FLOWERING SEASON: May into July. FLOWERS: white to bluish white with purple veining, few in short terminal clusters, about ³⁄₁₆" (4 mm) wide, tubular at the base with 4 unequal petal-like lobes. PLANT: 2–10" (5–25 cm) tall; leaves opposite, simple, oblong to oval, margin entire to indistinctly toothed, green. HABITAT: fields and waste areas.

Culver's-root
•*Veronicastrum virginicum* (L.) Farw.
•Figwort family **Scrophulariaceae**
FLOWERING SEASON: August. FLOWERS: white, many, in densely flowered slender 3–9" (7.5–22.5 cm) long terminal clus-

ters; individual flowers about ³⁄₁₆" (5 mm) long, tubular with 4 tiny lobes. PLANT: 2–7' (0.6–2.1 m) tall; leaves whorled in groups of 3 to 9, simple, lance-shaped, margin sharply toothed, green. HABITAT: moist meadows and woodlands.

Water-willow
•*Justicia americana* (L.) Vahl
•Acanthus family **Acanthaceae**
FLOWERING SEASON: July to early August. FLOWERS: white with violet markings, 2–4, in long-stalked axial clusters, about ½" (1.3 cm) long, tubular and 2-lipped; upper lip erect; lower lip with 3 large, spreading, petal-like lobes. PLANT: about 1–3' (30–90 cm) tall; leaves opposite, simple, long and narrow, margin entire, green. HABITAT: aquatic (in shallow water).

Buttonbush
•*Cephalanthus occidentalis* L.
•Madder family **Rubiaceae**
FLOWERING SEASON: mid-July to mid-August. FLOWERS: white, many, in densely flowered, 1" (2.5 cm) wide spherical terminal flowerheads, about ⁷⁄₁₆" (1.1 cm) long, tubular with 4 tiny, sharply pointed lobes. PLANT: shrub, 3–12' (0.9–4 m) tall; leaves whorled or opposite, simple, ovate with a pointed tip, margin entire, green. HABITAT: swamps and moist meadows.

Thyme Leaf Speedwell / *Veronica serpyllifolia*

Buttonbush / *Cephalanthus occidentalis*

Culver's-root / *Veronicastrum virginicum*

Water-willow / *Justicia americana*

Cow-wheat / *Melampyrum lineare*

Turtle-heads / *Chelone glabra*

White Snakeroot
•*Eupatorium rugosum* Houtt.
•Aster family **Asteraceae**
FLOWERING SEASON: mid-July to mid-September. **FLOWERS**: white, many, in dense, flat-topped terminal clusters; individual flowerheads up to ³⁄₁₆" (5 mm) long, filamentous. **PLANT**: 1–5' (0.3–1.5 m) tall; leaves opposite, simple, ovate with a pointed tip, margin toothed, green. **HABITAT**: woodlands.

Boneset
•*Eupatorium perfoliatum* L.
•Aster family **Asteraceae**
FLOWERING SEASON: August to late September. **FLOWERS**: white, many, in dense terminal clusters; individual flowerheads about ¼" (6 mm) long, filamentous. **PLANT**: 2–5' (0.6–1.5 m) tall; leaves opposite, simple, joined and perfoliate at the base, lance-shaped, margin toothed, green. **HABITAT**: wet soil in fields, roadsides, and waste areas.

White Snakeroot / *Eupatorium rugosum*

Boneset / *Eupatorium perfoliatum*

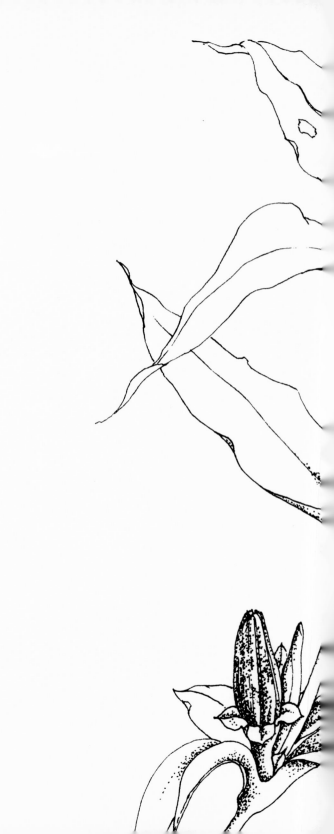

PART TWO

PINK TO RED FLOWERS
INCLUDING REDDISH PURPLE

❧

FLOWERS SYMMETRICAL, WITH 3 PETALS OR PETAL-LIKE PARTS

LEAVES WHORLED, SIMPLE

Purple Trillium
• *Trillium erectum* L.
• Lily family **Liliaceae**
FLOWERING SEASON: late April through May. FLOWER: purplish red, solitary, terminal on an erect stalk, about 2½" (6.3 cm) wide, with 3 evenly whorled petals; petals lance-shaped, often slightly recurved. PLANT: 8–16" (20–40 cm) tall; leaves 3 in a whorl at the base of the flower stalk, simple, broadly ovate with a pointed tip, stalkless, margin entire, green. HABITAT: woodlands. COMMENTS: a form with greenish-yellow petals is fairly common. Odor unpleasant, like a wet dog.

FLOWERS SYMMETRICAL, WITH 4 PETALS OR PETAL-LIKE PARTS

LEAVES ALTERNATE, SIMPLE

Dame's Rocket
• *Hesperis matronalis* L.
• Mustard family **Brassicaceae**
FLOWERING SEASON: late May through June. FLOWERS: white, pink, purplish or variegated, many, in axial and terminal clusters, about ¾" (2 cm) wide, cross-shaped, with 4 rounded petals. PLANT: 2–3' (60–90 cm) tall; leaves alternate, simple, broadly lance-shaped, margin minutely toothed, green; seed pods up to 4" (10 cm) long, slender. HABITAT: fields, roadsides, waste areas, and woodlands.

Daphne
• *Daphne mezereum* L.
• Mezereum family **Thymelaeaceae**
FLOWERING SEASON: mid-April to early May. FLOWERS: rose-purple to occasionally white, many, in clusters of 2 to 5 along the branches, about ½" (1.3 cm) long, tubular with 4 spreading, petal-like lobes; pleasantly fragrant. PLANT: shrub, 1–4' (0.3–1.2 m) tall; leaves alternate and mostly clustered near branch tips, simple, lance-shaped, margin entire, green. HABITAT: moist woodlands.

Fireweed
• *Epilobium angustifolium* L.
• Evening Primrose family **Onagraceae**
FLOWERING SEASON: mid-July through August. FLOWERS: pinkish purple, many in a slender, pyramid-shaped terminal cluster, about 1" (2.5 cm) wide, with 4 rounded, unequal petals. PLANT: 2–8' (0.6–2.4 m) tall; leaves alternate, simple, lance-shaped, margin entire, green. HABITAT: roadsides, fields, or recently disturbed or burned areas.

Great Hairy Willow-herb
• *Epilobium hirsutum* L.
• Evening Primrose family **Onagraceae**
FLOWERING SEASON: mid-July through August. FLOWERS: rose-purple, several in a terminal cluster, about 1" (2.5 cm) wide, with 4 rounded, distinctly notched petals. PLANT: 2–5' (0.6–1.5 m) tall; leaves alternate, simple, lance-shaped, margin sharply toothed, green. HABITAT: open moist areas and waste areas.

Daphne / *Daphne mezereum*

Purple Trillium / *Trillium erectum*

Great Hairy Willow-herb / *Epilobium hirsutum*

Fireweed / *Epilobium angustifolium*

Dame's Rocket / *Hesperis matronalis*

FLOWERS SYMMETRICAL, WITH 5 PETALS OR PETAL-LIKE PARTS

LEAVES BASAL, SIMPLE

Pitcher-plant
•*Sarracenia purpurea* L.
•Pitcher-plant family **Sarraceniaceae**
FLOWERING SEASON: June. FLOWER: purplish red with a yellowish shield-like center, solitary, terminal, about 2" (5 cm) wide, with 5 obovate petals that are narrowed in the middle, nodding. PLANT: 8–24" (20–60 cm) tall; leaves basal, simple, tubular, pitcher-like with downward-pointing stiff hairs on the inner surface, green to red with purple veining. HABITAT: bogs and fens. COMMENTS: a carnivorous plant.

Pink Pyrola
•*Pyrola asarifolia* Michx.
•Shinleaf family **Pyrolaceae**
FLOWERING SEASON: mid-June to mid-July. FLOWERS: rose to pale purple, several to many in a spike-like terminal cluster, about ⅝" (1.6 cm) wide, with 5 rounded petals, nodding. PLANT: 5–10" (12.5–25 cm) tall; leaves basal, simple, broadly kidney-shaped to nearly round, margin minutely toothed, green. HABITAT: moist woodlands, swamps, and fens. COMMENTS: *endangered. Do not disturb.*

LEAVES ALTERNATE, SIMPLE

Smartweed
•*Polygonum pensylvanicum* L.
•Buckwheat family **Polygonaceae**
FLOWERING SEASON: August-September. FLOWERS: pinkish white to rose, many in densely flowered, cylindrical terminal clusters, minute with 5 petal-like lobes. PLANT: 1–3' (30–90 cm) tall; leaves alternate, simple, lance-shaped, margin entire, green. HABITAT: fields, cultivated ground, and moist soil. COMMENTS: many species of smartweed, some with arrow-head-shaped leaves and painfully prickly stems, are found in this region.

Water Smartweed
•*Polygonum amphibium* L.
•Buckwheat family **Polygonaceae**
FLOWERING SEASON: July into August. FLOWERS: rose-pink, many in an erect ovoid to cylindrical terminal cluster, minute, with 5 petal-like lobes. PLANT: usually aquatic, stem 4–20" long; leaves alternate, erect on stem or floating, simple; erect leaves broadly lance-shaped with a round base; floating leaves broader; margin entire, green. HABITAT: shallow water in ponds, lakes, and swamps.

Hardhack
•*Spiraea tomentosa* L.
•Rose family **Rosaceae**
FLOWERING SEASON: mid-July to mid-August. FLOWERS: rosy pink, many in upright 3–5" (7.5–12.5 cm) tall upper axial and terminal clusters, about ⁵⁄₁₆" (8 mm) wide, with 5 rounded petals. PLANT: shrub, 2–4' (0.6–1.2 m) tall; leaves alternate, simple, oval to oblong, margin coarsely and unevenly toothed, green, woolly on the lower surface. HABITAT: swamps and open moist ground.

Pink Pyrola / *Pyrola asarifolia*

Pitcher-plant / *Sarracenia purpurea*

Water Smartweed / *Polygonum amphibium*

Smartweed / *Polygonum pensylvanicum*

Hardhack / *Spiraea tomentosa*

Purple-flowering Raspberry
•*Rubus odoratus* L.
•Rose family **Rosaceae**
FLOWERING SEASON: June-July. FLOWERS: pink to pale purple, few to several, in terminal and upper axial clusters, 1–2" (2.5–5 cm) wide, with 5 rounded petals. PLANT: shrub, 2–5' (0.6–1.5 m) tall; leaves alternate, simple, maple-like, 3 to 5-lobed; lobes pointed, margins irregularly toothed, green; upper limbs coated with purplish hairs. HABITAT: along the edges of woods, streams, trails, and roadsides.

Lapland Rosebay
•*Rhododendron lapponicum* (L.) Wahl.
•Heath family **Ericaceae**
FLOWERING SEASON: June. FLOWERS: pinkish purple, usually 1 to 4 in a loose terminal cluster, about ¾" (1.9 cm) wide, tubular at the base with 5 spreading, petal-like lobes. PLANT: mostly prostrate; leaves alternate, mostly clustered near the tips of woody stems, simple, lance-shaped with an entire margin, green, evergreen. HABITAT: alpine regions. COMMENTS: *endangered. Do not disturb.*

Live-forever
•*Sedum telephium* L.
•Sedum family **Crassulaceae**
FLOWERING SEASON: August-September. FLOWERS: pinkish red to reddish purple, many in flat-topped, rounded terminal clusters, about ¼" (6 mm) wide, with 5 lance-shaped petals. PLANT: 12–18" (30–45 cm) tall; leaves alternate, simple, ovate, thick and fleshy, margin coarsely toothed, light green. HABITAT: fields, roadsides, and moist areas.

LEAVES ALTERNATE, COMPOUND OR DEEPLY DIVIDED

Musk-mallow
•*Malva moschata* L.
•Mallow family **Malvaceae**
FLOWERING SEASON: mid-June through July. FLOWERS: pink or white, often with lavender veins, several, most in terminal clusters, 1½–2" (3.8–5 cm) wide, with 5 broad petals notched at the tip. PLANT: 1–2' (30–60 cm) tall; leaves alternate, simple, with 5 deeply cut and subdivided lobes, green. HABITAT: fields, roadsides, and waste areas.

Sea-beach Rose, Salt-spray Rose
•*Rosa rugosa* Thunb.
•Rose family **Rosaceae**
FLOWERING SEASON: July-August. FLOWERS: dark rose-pink to rose-lavender with a yellow center, solitary to several in leaf axils, 2–3" (5–7.5 cm) wide, with 5 rounded petals, fragrant. PLANT: shrub, 2–5' (0.6–1.5 m) tall; leaves alternate, pinnately compound with 5 to 9 leaflets; leaflets elliptic to oblong, margins toothed, green; stem very spiny and hairy; fruit a large, rounded red hip. HABITAT: thickets, sand dunes, and roadsides near the ocean.

Purple-flowering Raspberry / *Rubus odoratus*

Sea-beach Rose, Salt-spray Rose / *Rosa rugosa*

Lapland Rosebay / *Rhododendron lapponicum*

Musk-mallow / *Malva moschata*

Live-forever / *Sedum telephium*

Purple Avens, Water Avens

• *Geum rivale* L.
• Rose family **Rosaceae**

FLOWERING SEASON: mid-May to mid-June. FLOWERS: purple, few in a loose terminal cluster, ¾–1" (1.9–2.5 cm) wide, urn-shaped, with 5 rounded petals, nodding. PLANT: about 1–3' (30–90 cm) tall; leaves alternate, pinnately compound; leaflets ovate to lance-shaped, margins toothed, green. HABITAT: swamps and low moist ground.

Purple Cinquefoil, Marsh Cinquefoil

• *Potentilla palustris* (L.) Scop.
• Rose family **Rosaceae**

FLOWERING SEASON: July. FLOWERS: purple, solitary to several, terminal or axillary, ¾–1¼" (1.9–3.1 cm) wide, with 5 tiny petals alternating with 5 larger pointed, petal-like sepals. PLANT: trailing, up to 2' (60 cm) or more long; leaves alternate, pinnately compound; leaflets oblong to oval, margins toothed, green. HABITAT: swamps, fens, and bogs.

LEAVES OPPOSITE OR WHORLED, SIMPLE

Deptford Pink

• *Dianthus armeria* L.
• Pink family **Caryophyllaceae**

FLOWERING SEASON: mid-June to early August. FLOWERS: pink with white dots, one to few, in small terminal groups, about ½" (1.3 cm) wide, with 5 elliptical petals that are finely toothed at the tips. PLANT: 6–18" (15–45 cm) tall; leaves opposite, simple, long and narrow, margin entire, green. HABITAT: fields and woodland edges.

Maiden Pink

• *Dianthus deltoides* L.
• Pink family **Caryophyllaceae**

FLOWERING SEASON: August. FLOWERS:

reddish pink with a red-rimmed central eye, solitary to few, terminal, about ½" (1.3 cm) wide, with 5 petals, tips of petals coarsely toothed. PLANT: 6–15" (15–46 cm) tall; leaves opposite, simple, narrowly lance-shaped, margin entire, green. HABITAT: waste areas and meadows.

Ragged-robin

• *Lychnis flos-cuculi* L.
• Pink family **Caryophyllaceae**

FLOWERING SEASON: late May to mid-June. FLOWERS: pink, several to many, in terminal and upper axial clusters, about ¾" (1.9 cm) wide, with 5 petals, each petal cleft into 4 long narrow lobes. PLANT: 1–2' (30–60 cm) tall; leaves basal and opposite, simple, narrowly lance-shaped, margin entire, green. HABITAT: moist fields and meadows.

Bog Laurel

• *Kalmia polifolia* Wang.
• Heath family **Ericaceae**

FLOWERING SEASON: late May to mid-June. FLOWERS: pale pink, several in a loose terminal cluster, about ¾" (2 cm) wide, broadly saucer-shaped, with 5 pointed lobes. PLANT: shrub, 6–24" (15.5–61 cm) tall; leaves opposite or in whorls of 3, simple, narrowly oblong with an entire margin, green, evergreen. HABITAT: bogs and fens.

Purple Cinquefoil, Marsh Cinquefoil / *Potentilla palustris*

Ragged-robin / *Lychnis flos-cuculi*

Maiden Pink / *Dianthus deltoides*

Deptford Pink / *Dianthus armeria*

Purple Avens, Water Avens / *Geum rivale*

Bog Laurel / *Kalmia polifolia*

Sheep Laurel, Lambkill
- *Kalmia angustifolia* L.
- Heath family **Ericaceae**

FLOWERING SEASON: late May to early July. FLOWERS: dark reddish pink, many in a spherical cluster on the upper portion of the stems, about ½" (1.3 cm) wide, saucer-shaped with 5 shallowly pointed lobes. PLANT: shrub, 6–36" (15–90 cm) tall; leaves opposite or in whorls of 3, simple, narrowly oblong with an entire margin, green, evergreen. HABITAT: in moist soils along woodlands, swamps, and fens. COMMENTS: the alternate common name lambkill refers to the *poisonous* nature of this plant.

Alpine Azalea
- *Loiseleuria procumbens* (L.) Desv.
- Heath family **Ericaceae**

FLOWERING SEASON: June. FLOWERS: pink to white, 1 to 5 in loose terminal groups, about ³⁄₁₆" (5 mm) long, short-tubular with 5 large triangular lobes. PLANT: nearly prostrate; leaves mostly opposite along a woody stem, simple, narrowly elliptic with an incurved margin, green, evergreen. HABITAT: alpine regions. COMMENTS: *endangered. Do not disturb.*

Wild Geranium
- *Geranium maculatum* L.
- Geranium family **Geraniaceae**

FLOWERING SEASON: mid-May to mid-June. FLOWERS: rose-purple to occasionally white, 1 to 3 in loose terminal clusters, about 1¼" (3.1 cm) wide, with 5 rounded petals. PLANT: 1–2' (30–60 cm) tall; leaves basal and opposite along the stem, simple, deeply divided into 5 lobes, margin unevenly toothed, green. HABITAT: woodlands.

Common Milkweed
- *Asclepias syriaca* L.
- Milkweed family **Asclepiadaceae**

FLOWERING SEASON: late June to mid-July. FLOWERS: greenish, purple to pinkish white, many, in rounded terminal or upper axial clusters, about ⅜" (1 cm) wide, with 5 deeply recurved petals and a 5-pointed crown-like center. PLANT: 3–5' (0.9–1.5 m) tall; leaves opposite, simple, oblong, margin entire, green. HABITAT: fields and waste areas. COMMENTS: most species of milkweed exude a milky white latex when cut.

Swamp Milkweed
- *Asclepias incarnata* L.
- Milkweed family **Asclepiadaceae**

FLOWERING SEASON: July-August. FLOWERS: red to rose-purple, many in a rounded terminal cluster, about ¼" (6 mm) wide, with 5 deeply recurved petals and a 5-pointed crown-like center. PLANT: 2–4' (0.6–1.2 m) tall; leaves opposite, simple, narrowly lance-shaped, margin entire, green. HABITAT: swamps, moist meadows, and along bodies of water.

Spreading Dogbane
- *Apocynum androsaemifolium* L.
- Dogbane family **Apocynaceae**

FLOWERING SEASON: late June through July. FLOWERS: pink, several to many, in loose terminal or axial clusters, about ⁵⁄₁₆" (8 mm) wide, bell-shaped with 5 tooth-like lobes. PLANT: 1–4' (0.3–1.2 m) tall; leaves opposite, simple, oval, margin entire, green. HABITAT: moist fields and meadows. COMMENTS: plant exudes a milky white latex when cut.

Sheep Laurel, Lambkill / *Kalmia angustifolia*

Alpine Azalea / *Loiseleuria procumbens*

Common Milkweed / *Asclepias syriaca*

Wild Geranium / *Geranium maculatum*

Spreading Dogbane / *Apocynum androsaemifolium*

Swamp Milkweed / *Asclepias incarnata*

Summer Phlox

- *Phlox paniculata* L.
- Phlox family **Polemoniaceae**

FLOWERING SEASON: mid-July into September. FLOWERS: pink, purple, or white, many in dense, rounded terminal and axial clusters, about 1" (2.5 cm) wide, tubular with 5 nearly round, overlapping, petal-like lobes; fragrant. PLANT: 2–5' (0.6–1.5 m) tall; leaves opposite, simple, lance-shaped, margin entire, green. HABITAT: meadows and open woodlots. COMMENTS: wild sweet-William, *Phlox maculata*, is a shorter plant with smaller flowers and purple-spotted stems.

Moss Phlox

- *Phlox subulata* L.
- Phlox family **Polemoniaceae**

FLOWERING SEASON: early to mid-May. FLOWERS: pink, purple or white, many in terminal clusters, about ¾" (2 cm) wide, tubular with 5 notched triangular petal-like lobes. PLANT: 2–5" (5–12.5 cm) tall, forming dense mats; leaves whorled, simple, short and very narrow, margin entire, green. HABITAT: rocky soils, hillsides, and cliffs.

Twinflower

- *Linnaea borealis* L.
- Honeysuckle family **Caprifoliaceae**

FLOWERING SEASON: mid-June to mid-July. FLOWERS: pinkish, in pairs on tall terminal stalks, about ⁷⁄₁₆" (1.1 cm) long, bell-shaped with 5 petal-like lobes, nodding. PLANT: prostrate; leaves opposite on 6–15" (15–37.5 cm) long stems, simple, ovate, margin scalloped, green. HABITAT: woodland clearings, shaded fens, and along woodland streams.

LEAVES OPPOSITE, DEEPLY DIVIDED

Herb-Robert

- *Geranium robertianum* L.
- Geranium family **Geraniaceae**

FLOWERING SEASON: late May into September. FLOWERS: dark pink to reddish purple, several in pairs on axial stalks, about ½" (1.3 cm) wide, with 5 rounded petals. PLANT: 6–18" (15–45 cm) tall; leaves opposite, deeply and repeatedly divided, margins finely lobed or toothed, green. HABITAT: woodlands.

FLOWERS SYMMETRICAL, WITH 6 PETALS OR PETAL-LIKE PARTS

LEAVES ALTERNATE, SIMPLE

Twisted-stalk, Rose Mandarin

- *Streptopus roseus* Michx.
- Lily family **Liliaceae**

FLOWERING SEASON: mid-May to early June. FLOWERS: purplish rose, several, found singly or occasionally paired in axils, about ½" (1.3 cm) long, bell-shaped with 6 sharply pointed often recurved tips, pendant. PLANT: 1–2½' (30–75 cm) tall; leaves alternate along an angularly twisted stalk, simple, lance-shaped with a rounded base slightly clasping the stem, margin entire, green. HABITAT: moist woodlands. COMMENTS: the common name twisted-stalk refers to the zigzag appearance of the stalk.

LEAVES OPPOSITE OR WHORLED, SIMPLE

Swamp Loosestrife

- *Decodon verticillatus* (L.) Ell.
- Loosestrife family **Lythraceae**

FLOWERING SEASON: August. FLOWERS: pinkish purple, many, in crowded axial clusters, about 1" (2.5 cm) wide, with 6 narrow petals. PLANT: 3–10' (0.9–3 m) tall; leaves whorled, simple, narrowly lance-shaped, margin entire, green. HABITAT: swamps.

Herb-Robert / *Geranium robertianum*

Moss Phlox / *Phlox subulata*

Swamp Loosestrife / *Decodon verticillatus*

Twinflower / *Linnaea borealis*

Summer Phlox / *Phlox paniculata*

Twisted-stalk, Rose Mandarin / *Streptopus roseus*

Purple Loosestrife

•*Lythrum salicaria* L.

•Loosestrife family **Lythraceae**

FLOWERING SEASON: July into August. **FLOWERS:** purplish pink to reddish purple, many in tall, slender terminal clusters, about ⅝" (1.6 cm) wide, with 6 petals. **PLANT:** 2–4' (0.6–1.2 m) tall; leaves mostly opposite, simple, lance-shaped, margin entire, green. **HABITAT:** swamps, roadsides, and moist soils. **COMMENTS:** an introduced ornamental that has become a serious wetland invader.

~

FLOWERS SYMMETRICAL, WITH 7 OR MORE PETALS OR PETAL-LIKE PARTS

LEAVES ALTERNATE, SIMPLE

Common Fleabane, Philadelphia Fleabane

•*Erigeron philadelphicus* L.

•Aster family **Asteraceae**

FLOWERING SEASON: April–August. **FLOWERHEADS:** white to pink with a yellow center, several to numerous, in terminal and upper axial clusters, individual flowerheads about ¾" (2 cm) wide, rimmed with 100–150 narrow petal-like rays. **PLANT:** 1–3' (30–91 cm) tall; leaves alternate, simple, of two types; basal and lower leaves spathulate to obovate, somewhat hairy; upper leaves clasping, with a heart-shaped base, somewhat hairy; margin toothed, green; stems hairy. **HABITAT:** fields, woodlands, and waste areas.

Robin's-plantain

•*Erigeron pulchellus* Michx.

•Aster family **Asteraceae**

FLOWERING SEASON: late May to early June. **FLOWERHEADS:** pale violet or purplish with a yellow center, flowerheads 1 to 6 in a terminal cluster, individual flowerheads 1–1½" (2.5–3.8 cm) wide, rimmed with numerous very narrow, petal-like rays. **PLANT:** 10–24" (25–60 cm) tall; leaves alternate and basal, simple to lance-shaped, margin finely toothed, green. **HABITAT:** open woodlands and shaped roadsides.

New England Aster

•*Aster novae-angliae* L.

•Aster family **Asteraceae**

FLOWERING SEASON: mid-August into October. **FLOWERHEADS:** violet-purple with a yellow center, flowerheads many, termi-nal and upper axial, individual flowerheads 1–2" (2.5–5 cm) wide, rimmed with 40 to 50 petal-like rays. **PLANT:** 2–8' (0.6–2.4 m) tall; leaves alternate, simple, lance-shaped, margin entire, green. **HABITAT:** meadows, roadsides, and along swamps.

LEAVES OPPOSITE, DEEPLY DIVIDED

Field Scabious, Bluebuttons

•*Knautia arvensis* (L.) Coulter

•Teasel family **Dipsacaceae**

FLOWERING SEASON: June-July. **FLOWER-HEADS:** lilac-purple, many, terminal and upper axial, individual flowerheads about 1¼" (3.1 cm) wide, composed of many multilobed petal-like rays. **PLANT:** 1–3' (30–90 cm) tall; leaves basal or opposite, simple, lance-shaped to 5–7 lobed, margin entire, green. **HABITAT:** fields and waste areas.

Common Fleabane, Philadelphia Fleabane / *Erigeron philadelphicus*

Purple Loosestrife / *Lythrum salicaria*

New England Aster / *Aster novae-angliae*

Robin's-plantain / *Erigeron pulchellus*

Field Scabious, Bluebuttons / *Knautia arvensis*

FLOWERS NOT RADIALLY SYMMETRICAL, MINUTE, FILAMENTOUS, TUBULAR WITH NO PETAL-LIKE LOBES, OR WITH NO OBVIOUS PETAL-LIKE PARTS

LEAF ABSENT OR TYPICALLY LACKING AT FLOWERING

Pinesap, False Beechdrops
• *Monotropa hypopithys* L.
• Indian-pipe family **Monotropaceae**
FLOWERING SEASON: July-August. **FLOWERS:** white, yellowish or pink, several in a 1-sided terminal cluster, about ½" (1.3 cm) long, appearing tubular, with usually 5 slightly flaring tips, nodding. **PLANT:** 4–12" (10–30 cm) tall; leaves absent; stalk with numerous tiny leaf-like bracts, white, yellowish, or pink. **HABITAT:** woodlands.

Arethusa, Dragon's Mouth
• *Arethusa bulbosa* L.
• Orchid family **Orchidaceae**
FLOWERING SEASON: mid- to late June. **FLOWER:** rose-magenta, solitary, terminal; about 1¾" (4.5 cm) tall, with 5 somewhat erect narrowly lance-shaped petals and sepals and a downward curved lip; lip oblong with a wrinkled margin, white with pinkish margins and a tuft of white to yellow hairs. **PLANT:** 5–10" (13–25 cm) tall; leaf solitary, on the lower stem, simple, long and narrow but not developed at flowering, margin entire, green. **HABITAT:** sphagnum fens.

LEAVES BASAL, SIMPLE

Calypso, Fairy Slipper
• *Calypso bulbosa* (L.) Oakes
• Orchid family **Orchidaceae**
FLOWERING SEASON: late May to early June. **FLOWER:** rose-pink with a tuft of yellow hairs, solitary, terminal; about 1¾" (4.5 cm) tall, with 5 erect narrowly lance-shaped petals and sepals and a pendent lip; lip white with purplish markings and a conspicuous tuft of yellow hairs. **PLANT:** 3–6" (7.5–15.5 cm)

tall; leaf solitary, basal, simple, nearly round, margin entire, green. **HABITAT:** white cedar, *Thuja occidentalis*, swamps. **COMMENTS:** *endangered. Do not disturb.*

Moccasin Flower, Pink Lady's Slipper
• *Cypripedium acaule* Ait.
• Orchid family **Orchidaceae**
FLOWERING SEASON: late May through June. **FLOWER:** lip pink, sepals and petals light purplish brown; solitary, terminal; lip about 2" (5 cm) long and pouch-like, pendant. **PLANT:** 6–12" (15–30 cm) tall; leaves 2, basal, simple, broadly oblong, margin entire, green. **HABITAT:** variable, from dry coniferous or mixed woods to sphagnum fens.

Showy Orchis
• *Galearis spectabilis* (L.) Raf.
• Orchid family **Orchidaceae**
FLOWERING SEASON: late May through late June. **FLOWERS:** bicolored, pale purplish and white, 3 to 6 on a slender terminal cluster, about 1" (2.5 cm) tall; 5 sepals and petals, pale purplish, overlapping and hood-like; lip white, pendant, obovate with a prominent spur. **PLANT:** 4–12" (10–30 cm) tall; leaves 2, basal, simple, obovate, margin entire, green. **HABITAT:** woodlands.

Calopogon, Grass Pink
• *Calopogon tuberosus* (L.) BSP.
• Orchid family **Orchidaceae**
FLOWERING SEASON: late June through late July. **FLOWERS:** pink to rose pink, 3 to 15 in a slender terminal cluster, about 1¼" (3.1 cm) tall and wide, with 5 oblong to obovate petals and sepals and an erect lip; lip narrow, triangular-tipped, with a conspicuous tuft of white-to yellow-tipped hairs. **PLANT:** 1–2½' (30–76 cm) tall; leaf usually

Arethusa, Dragon's Mouth / *Arethusa bulbosa*

Calopogon, Grass Pink / *Calopogon tuberosus*

Calypso, Fairy Slipper / *Calypso bulbosa*

Pinesap, False Beechdrops / *Monotropa hypopithys*

Moccasin Flower, Pink Lady's Slipper / *Cypripedium acaule*

Showy Orchis / *Galearis spectabilis*

solitary, basal, simple, long and narrow, green, margin entire. HABITAT: sphagnum fens.

Lily-leaved Twayblade
• *Liparis lilifolia (Linnaeus)*
  L.C. Richard ex Ker
• Orchid family **Orchidaceae**
FLOWERING SEASON: June to early July. FLOWERS: mauve to pale purple, 10–20 in a loosely flowered terminal cluster, about ¾" (2 cm) long, with 5 very narrow petals and sepals and a large egg-shaped lip. PLANT: 4–10" (10–25 cm) tall; leaves 2, basal, simple, broadly egg-shaped, margin entire, green. HABITAT: moist woods and thickets. COMMENTS: *endangered. Do not disturb.* Within the area covered by this book, currently known only from remote populations in Vermont.

LEAVES ALTERNATE, SIMPLE

Early Azalea
• *Rhododendron prinophyllum* (Small) Millais
• Heath family **Ericaceae**
FLOWERING SEASON: mid-May to mid-June. FLOWERS: pale pink, several in a terminal cluster, about 2" (5 cm) long, tubular at the base with 5 unequal and widely flaring lobes, extremely fragrant. PLANT: shrub, 2–6' (0.6–1.8 m) tall; leaves alternate, mostly clustered at the tips of the stems, usually emerging with or shortly after the flowers, simple, lance-shaped with an entire margin, green. HABITAT: along streams, fens, and mountainous woodlands. COMMENTS: frequently attacked by a fungus called *Exobasidium rhododendri,* which transforms some leaves into fleshy fruit-like structures.

Rhodora
• *Rhododendron canadense* (L.) Torr.
• Heath family **Ericaceae**

FLOWERING SEASON: May-June. FLOWERS: magenta, several in showy terminal clusters, about 1" (2.5 cm) long, tubular at the base with 2 extended lobes; upper lobe long and narrow with 3 shallow tips; lower lobe deeply divided. PLANT: shrub, 1–3' (30–92 cm) tall; leaves alternate, clustered near the tips of the stems, usually emerging after the flowers, simple, oblong with an entire margin, green. HABITAT: fens and damp hillsides.

Mountain Cranberry
• *Vaccinum vitis-ideae* L. var. minus Lodd.
• Heath family **Ericaceae**
FLOWERING SEASON: June-July. FLOWERS: pinkish red, several in small terminal clusters; individual flowers about ¼" (6 mm) long, waxy, tubular, with tiny teeth. PLANT: low shrub, prostrate or up to 8" (20 cm) tall; leaves alternate, simple, oval, margin entire, green, glossy, evergreen. HABITAT: rocky mountain slopes and alpine areas.

Fringed Polygala, Gaywings
• *Polygala paucifolia* Willd.
• Milkwort family **Polygalaceae**
FLOWERING SEASON: mid-May to early June. FLOWERS: rose-purple, 1 to 4, axial in the upper leaves, about ¾" (1.9 cm) long, appearing tubular with a fringed tip and two petal-like lateral sepals. PLANT: 4–7" (10–17.5 cm) tall; leaves alternate, simple, ovate with a pointed tip, margin entire, green. HABITAT: woodlands.

Comfrey
• *Symphytum officinale* L.
• Borage family **Boraginaceae**
FLOWERING SEASON: late May through July. FLOWERS: purple or yellow, many, in arched, typically terminal clusters, about ¾" (1.9 cm) long, tubular with 5 tiny lobes. PLANT: 2–3' (60–90 cm) tall;

Comfrey / *Symphytum officinale*

Mountain Cranberry / *Vaccinum vitis-ideae*

Fringed Polygala, Gaywings / *Polygala paucifolia*

Rhodora / *Rhododendron canadense*

Lily-leaved Twayblade / *Liparis lilifolia*

Early Azalea / *Rhododendron prinophyllum*

leaves alternate, simple, lance-shaped, hairy, margin entire, green. **HABITAT:** meadows and waste areas.

Cardinal Flower
- *Lobelia cardinalis* L.
- Bluebell family **Campanulaceae**

FLOWERING SEASON: mid-July through August. **FLOWERS:** scarlet, several to many in a showy, slender terminal cluster, about 1¼" (3.1 cm) long, tubular at the base, with 5 unequal, spreading, petal-like divisions. **PLANT:** 2–4½' (0.6–1.4 m) tall; leaves alternate, simple, lance-shaped, margin toothed, green. **HABITAT:** moist meadows, swamps, and edges of large bodies of water.

Common Burdock
- *Arctium minus* (Hill) Bernh.
- Aster family **Asteraceae**

FLOWERING SEASON: mid-July through August. **FLOWERHEADS:** pink to lavender, several to many in upper leaf axils, individual flowerheads ½–¾" (1.3–1.9 cm) wide, rounded, surrounded by spiny green bracts. **PLANT:** 3–5' (1–1.5 m) tall; leaves alternate, simple, broadly ovate, heart-shaped near the base, margin entire, green. **HABITAT:** roadsides and waste areas.

Black Knapweed
- *Centaurea nigra* L.
- Aster family **Asteraceae**

FLOWERING SEASON: July-August. **FLOWERHEADS:** rose-purple, solitary to several, terminal, rounded, individual flowerheads about 1" (2.5 cm) wide, base of flowerhead somewhat spherical, covered with deeply fringed, black-tipped bracts. **PLANT:** 1–2' (30–60 cm) tall; leaves alternate and basal, simple, oblong to lance-shaped, margin shallowly toothed to nearly entire, green. **HABITAT:** fields, roadsides, and waste areas. **COMMENTS:** spotted knapweed, *Centaurea maculosa*, has many flowerheads and leaves with narrow, pinnately arranged lobes.

Rose Pogonia, Snake-mouth
- *Pogonia ophioglossoides* (L.) Juss.
- Orchid family **Orchidaceae**

FLOWERING SEASON: late June through mid-July. **FLOWER:** pink, solitary, about 1¼" (3.1 cm) tall and wide, with 5 lance-to paddle-shaped petals and sepals above the lip; lip oblong with a fringed margin, pink with a central tuft of yellowish hair-like projections. **PLANT:** 8–15" (20–37.5 cm) tall; leaf usually solitary, on the lower stem, simple, oblong to obovate, margin entire, green. **HABITAT:** sphagnum fens, moist meadows, and swamps.

LEAVES ALTERNATE, COMPOUND OR DEEPLY DIVIDED

Red Columbine
- *Aquilegia canadensis* L.
- Crowfoot family **Ranunculaceae**

FLOWERING SEASON: mid-May through June. **FLOWERS:** scarlet, one to several, terminal, 1–2" (2.5–5 cm) long, with 5 tubular petals displaying yellow coloration near the openings, nodding. **PLANT:** 1–2' (30–60 cm) tall; leaves alternate, compound with 3 to 9 leaflets; leaflets wedge-shaped and irregularly lobed, green. **HABITAT:** variable (e.g., rocky woodlands, wet cliffs, and roadsides), frequently near water.

Pink Corydalis
- *Corydalis sempervirens* (L.) Pers.
- Fumitory family **Fumariaceae**

FLOWERING SEASON: late May to June. **FLOWERS:** pink with a yellow tip, many, in usually 5–10 flowered axial and terminal clusters, about ½–¾" (1.3–2 cm) long, tubular with a rounded spur at the base. **PLANT:** 1–2' (30–61 cm) tall; leaves basal and alternate, pinnately divided into deeply cleft toothed sections, green. **HABITAT:** rocky soil.

Pink Corydalis / *Corydalis sempervirens*

Rose Pogonia, Snake-mouth / *Pogonia ophioglossoides*

Cardinal Flower / *Lobelia cardinalis*

Common Burdock / *Arctium minus*

Red Columbine / *Aquilegia canadensis*

Black Knapweed / *Centaurea nigra*

Crown-vetch

- *Coronilla varia* L.
- Bean family **Fabaceae**

FLOWERING SEASON: June through early August. **FLOWERS:** bicolored, pink and white, many in dense, clover-like axial clusters about 1" (2.5 cm) wide, individual flowers about ⅜" (9 mm) long, narrowly pea-like. **PLANT:** prostrate or ascending, up to 2' (60 cm) tall; leaves alternate, pinnately compound with 11 to 25 leaflets; leaflets oblong, margins entire, green. **HABITAT:** roadsides and waste areas.

Beach-pea

- *Lathyrus japonicus* Willd.
- Bean family **Fabaceae**

FLOWERING SEASON: June into August. **FLOWERS:** bicolored, pinkish purple to violet and white, many, 6 to 10 in axial clusters, up to 1" (2.5 cm) long, pea-like. **PLANT:** vine, 1–2' (30–60 cm) long; leaves alternate, pinnately compound with 6 to 12 leaflets; leaflets oval, margins entire, green. **HABITAT:** ocean beaches, sometimes along large lakes.

Everlasting-pea

- *Lathyrus latifolius* L.
- Bean family **Fabaceae**

FLOWERING SEASON: late June to early August. **FLOWERS:** purplish pink, white or bluish, many, several in dense axial clusters, about 1" (2.5 cm) long, pea-like. **PLANT:** climbing vine, 2–5' (0.6–1.5 m) long; leaves alternate, compound with 2 leaflets and a winged stalk; leaflets oval, margins entire, green. **HABITAT:** roadsides, thickets, and waste areas.

Red Clover

- *Trifolium pratense* L.
- Bean family **Fabaceae**

FLOWERING SEASON: late May into September. **FLOWERS:** pinkish red, many in 1" (2.5 cm) tall ovoid flowerheads, individual flowers about ½" (1.3 cm) long, narrow. **PLANT:** 6–24" (15–60 cm) tall; leaves alternate, compound with 3 leaflets; leaflets oval to oblong, margins nearly entire, green with pale green chevrons. **HABITAT:** fields and meadows.

Rabbit's-foot Clover

- *Trifolium arvense* Pollich.
- Bean family **Fabaceae**

FLOWERING SEASON: August into September. **FLOWERS:** pale grayish pink, many, in ½–1" (1.3–2.5 cm) tall, densely fuzzy cylindrical terminal flowerheads, individual flowers inconspicuous. **PLANT:** 6–18" (15–46 cm) tall; leaves alternate, compound with 3 leaflets; leaflets narrowly oblong, margin entire, green. **HABITAT:** fields and waste areas.

Bull-thistle

- *Cirsium vulgare* (Savi) Tenore
- Aster family **Asteraceae**

FLOWERING SEASON: mid-July through August. **FLOWERHEADS:** rose-purple, several, terminal and upper axial, individual flowerheads 1½–2" (3.8–5 cm) wide and high, filamentous, base of flowerhead urn-shaped and covered with numerous slender, spiny, yellow-tipped green bracts. **PLANT:** 2–5' (0.6–1.5 m) tall; leaves alternate, simple, deeply cleft, margin irregular, very sharply toothed and prickly, green. **HABITAT:** fields, roadsides, and waste areas.

Beach-pea / *Lathyrus japonicus*

Everlasting-pea / *Lathyrus latifolius*

Red Clover / *Trifolium pratense*

Crown-vetch / *Coronilla varia*

Rabbit's-foot Clover / *Trifolium arvense*

Bull-thistle / *Cirsium vulgare*

Canada Thistle

- *Cirsium arvense* (L.) Scop.
- Aster family **Asteraceae**

FLOWERING SEASON: late June through July. **FLOWERHEADS:** lavender to pale rose, many, terminal and upper axial, individual flowerheads about ¾" (1.9 cm) wide, filamentous, base of flowerhead somewhat spherical and covered with numerous slender, spiny, green bracts. **PLANT:** 1–3' (30–90 cm) tall; leaves alternate, simple, deeply cleft, margin irregular, very sharply toothed and prickly, green. **HABITAT:** fields and waste areas.

LEAVES OPPOSITE OR WHORLED, SIMPLE

Wild Basil

- *Clinopodium vulgare* L.
- Mint family **Lamiaceae**

FLOWERING SEASON: mid-June through September. **FLOWERS:** pink to purple, several to many in 1" (2.5 cm) wide terminal and axial clusters, about ⅜" (9 mm) long, tubular and 2-lipped; upper lip 3-lobed, lower lip 2-lobed. **PLANT:** 1–2' (30–60 cm) tall; leaves opposite on a square stem, simple, ovate, margin wavy, green. **HABITAT:** woodlands.

Peppermint

- *Mentha aquatica* x *spicata* = *M.* x *piperita* L.
- Mint family **Lamiaceae**

FLOWERING SEASON: early August into September. **FLOWERS:** lavender, many in whorled, terminal, spike-like clusters, about ¼" (6 mm) long, tubular, 4-lobed. **PLANT:** 1–3' (30–90 cm) tall; leaves opposite on a square purplish stem, simple, lance-shaped, margin toothed, green **HABITAT:** moist soils. **COMMENTS:** the highly fragrant leaves are the source of the well-known herbal tea.

Bee-balm

- *Monarda didyma* L.
- Mint family **Lamiaceae**

FLOWERING SEASON: July-August. **FLOWERS:** scarlet, many in a rounded terminal cluster, about 1¾" (4.4 cm) long, tubular with 2 elongated lips; upper lip 2-lobed; lower lip 3-lobed. **PLANT:** 2–3' (60–90 cm) tall; leaves opposite on a square stem, simple, broadly lance-shaped, margin toothed, green. **HABITAT:** moist, often shaded, soils. **COMMENTS:** a domesticated form is commonly cultivated and is frequently visited by hummingbirds.

Bergamot

- *Monarda fistulosa* L.
- Mint family **Lamiaceae**

FLOWERING SEASON: mid-July through August. **FLOWERS:** lavender, many, in one or more rounded terminal clusters, about 1¼" (3.1 cm) long, tubular with 2 elongated lips; upper lip 2-lobed, lower lip 3-lobed. **PLANT:** 2–3' (60–90 cm) tall; leaves opposite on a square stem, simple, lance-shaped to ovate with a pointed tip, margin toothed, green. **HABITAT:** dry meadows.

Purple Dead-nettle

- *Lamium purpureum* L.
- Mint family **Lamiaceae**

FLOWERING SEASON: May. **FLOWERS:** purple-red, several, in axillary and terminal clusters, up to ½" (1.3 cm) long, tubular with 2 lips; upper lip 2-lobed and hairy; lower lip 3-lobed. **PLANT:** 6–18" (15–45 cm) tall; leaves opposite on a square stem, simple, ovate on the upper portion, heart-shaped at the base, margin bluntly toothed, green. **HABITAT:** roadsides and waste areas.

Bergamot / *Monarda fistulosa*

Canada Thistle / *Cirsium arvense*

Bee-balm / *Monarda didyma*

Purple Dead-nettle / *Lamium purpureum*

Peppermint / *Mentha aquatica* x *spicata*

Wild Basil / *Clinopodium vulgare*

Marjoram

- *Origanum vulgare* L.
- Mint family **Lamiaceae**

FLOWERING SEASON: mid July to early September. FLOWERS: pink to purple or nearly white, many in dense, rounded, usually terminal clusters, small, tubular with 2 lips; upper lip entire or 2-lobed; lower lip 3-lobed. PLANT: 1–2½' (30–76 cm) tall; leaves opposite on a square stem, simple, ovate to nearly heart-shaped, margin entire, green. HABITAT: fields and meadows. COMMENT: marjoram is a less potent relative of culinary oregano.

Wild Thyme

- *Thymus pulegioides* L.
- Mint family **Lamiaceae**

FLOWERING SEASON: mid-July to early September. FLOWERS: purple, many, in rounded terminal and axial clusters, tiny, tubular with 2 lips; upper lip entire; lower lip 3-lobed. PLANT: prostrate and creeping, 4–12" (10–30 cm) long; leaves tiny, opposite on a square stem, simple, oblong, margin entire, green. HABITAT: roadsides and meadows. COMMENTS: thyme makes an excellent culinary seasoning.

Teasel

- *Dipsacus fullonum* L.
- Teasel family **Dipsacaceae**

FLOWERING SEASON: August. FLOWERS: lavender, many, on oval to cylindrical terminal flowerheads; individual flowers about ½" (1.3 cm) long, tubular with 4 tiny rounded lobes. PLANT: 3–6' (0.9–1.8 m) tall; leaves opposite on a spiny stem, simple, oblong to lance-shaped, prickly on the lower central vein, margin entire to bluntly toothed, green. HABITAT: fields and waste areas.

Joe-pye-weed, Red Boneset

- *Eupatorium purpureum* L.
- Aster family **Asteraceae**

FLOWERING SEASON: August to late September. FLOWERHEADS: pink to purplish pink, many, in dense terminal clusters, individual flowerheads about ⁵⁄₁₆" (8 mm) wide, filamentous. PLANT: 3–10' (0.9–3 m) tall; leaves in whorls of 3 to 6, simple, lance-shaped, margin toothed, green; stem mostly green. HABITAT: moist soil in roadsides, fields, swamps, and wood-land edges. COMMENTS: spotted joe-pye-weed, *Eupatorium maculatum*, is a very similar species with flat-topped flower clusters and a purple or purple-spotted stem.

Teasel / *Dipsacus fullonum*

Joe-pye-weed, Red Boneset / *Eupatorium purpureum*

Marjoram / *Origanum vulgare*

Wild Thyme / *Thymus pulegioides*

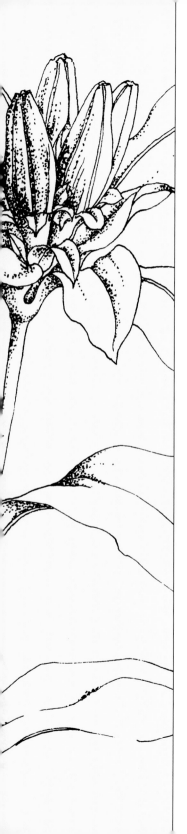

PART THREE

YELLOW TO ORANGE
FLOWERS

❧

FLOWERS SYMMETRICAL, WITH 3 PETALS OR PETAL-LIKE PARTS

LEAVES BASAL, SIMPLE

Northern Yellow-eyed Grass
- *Xyris montana* Ries
- Yellow-eyed Grass family **Xyridaceae**

FLOWERING SEASON: July. **FLOWERS:** yellow, one to few, terminal from a small cone-like head on a very slender stem, about ¼" (6 mm) wide, with 3 rounded, petal-like parts. **PLANT:** 2–12" (5–30 cm) tall; leaves mostly basal, simple, long and very narrow, margin entire, green. **HABITAT:** fens and bogs.

Yellow Iris, Yellow Flag
- *Iris pseudacorus* L.
- Iris family **Iridaceae**

FLOWERING SEASON: June through early July. **FLOWERS:** yellow, several, terminal on an upright stem, about 3¼" (8.1 cm) wide, perianth 6-parted, outer 3 parts obovate with down-turned tips, inner 3 parts smaller, oblong and nearly erect. **PLANT:** 1½–3' (45–90 cm) tall; leaves basal, simple, long and narrow, margin entire, bluish green. **HABITAT:** marshes, wet meadows, and along bodies of water. **COMMENTS:** because most individuals focus on the 3 prominent downturned petals and tend not to notice the 3 less conspicuous upright petals, we have placed this wildflower in this section.

FLOWERS SYMMETRICAL, WITH 4 PETALS OR PETAL-LIKE PARTS

LEAVES BASAL, COMPOUND

Wintercress
- *Barbarea vulgaris* R. Br. ex Ait.
- Mustard family **Brassicaceae**

FLOWERING SEASON: mid-May to mid-June. **FLOWERS:** yellow, several to many in axial and terminal clusters, about ⁵⁄₁₆" (8 mm) wide, cross-shaped, with 4 oval petals. **PLANT:** 1–2' (30–60 cm) tall; leaves alternate and basal, upper leaves usually with a few large teeth, basal leaves with a large, oval, toothless terminal division and 1 to 4 pairs of much smaller lobes along the stalk, green; seed pods about 1" (2.5 cm) long, slender, somewhat spreading. **HABITAT:** fields and waste areas. **COMMENTS:** Charlock, *Sinapis arvensis*, is 1–2' (30–60 cm) tall and has ⅝" (1.6 cm) long seed pods that are constricted around the circular seeds.

LEAVES ALTERNATE, SIMPLE

Witch-hazel
- *Hamamelis virginiana* L.
- Witch-hazel family **Hamamelidaceae**

FLOWERING SEASON: October. **FLOWERS:** yellow, many, in axillary clusters of 2 to several, about 1" (2.5 cm) wide, with 4 long and very narrow petals. **PLANT:** shrub, 5–25' (1.5–7.5 m) tall; leaves alternate, simple, oval with an asymmetrical base, margin with large rounded teeth, green. **HABITAT:** wooded swamps, moist woodlands.

Evening Primrose
- *Oenothera biennis* L.
- Evening Primrose family **Onagraceae**

FLOWERING SEASON: July-September. **FLOWERS:** yellow, several in a terminal cluster, about 1–2" (2.5–5 cm) wide, with 4 rounded, slightly notched petals. **PLANT:** 1–9' (0.3–2.7 m) tall; leaves alternate, simple, lance-shaped, margin slightly wavy, green. **HABITAT:** in dry, sunny soils such as roadsides and fields. **COMMENTS:** flowers open in early evening and remain open through the following morning.

Northern Yellow-eyed Grass / *Xyris montana*

Wintercress / *Barbarea vulgaris*

Witch-hazel / *Hamamelis virginiana*

Yellow Iris, Yellow Flag / *Iris pseudacorus*

Evening Primrose / *Oenothera biennis*

LEAVES ALTERNATE, COMPOUND OR DEEPLY DIVIDED

Celandine
- *Chelidonium majus* L.
- Poppy family **Papaveraceae**

FLOWERING SEASON: mid-May through June. FLOWERS: yellow, few to several, in loose terminal clusters, about ⅝" (1.6 cm) wide, with 4 rounded petals. PLANT: 1–2' (30–60 cm) tall; leaves alternate, appearing pinnately compound, margin unevenly bluntly toothed, green. HABITAT: moist places and woodlands. COMMENTS: the damaged plant exudes bright yellow sap.

Black Mustard
- *Brassica nigra* (L.) Koch
- Mustard family **Brassicaceae**

FLOWERING SEASON: June-July. FLOWERS: yellow, several to many in rounded terminal and axial clusters, about ⅜" (1 cm) wide, with 4 rounded petals. PLANT: 2–7' (0.6–2.2 m) tall; leaves alternate, pinately compound; upper leaflet large and often lobed; lower leaflets few, small; margin toothed, green; seedpods about ½" (1.3 cm) long, tightly appressed to the stem. HABITAT: fields and waste areas. COMMENTS: the seeds may be used to produce a pungent, hot mustard.

Creeping Yellow-cress
- *Rorippa sylvestris* (L.) Besser
- Mustard family **Brassicaceae**

FLOWERING SEASON: June to mid-August. FLOWERS: yellow, several to many, in slender terminal clusters, about ¼" (6 mm) wide, with 4 rounded petals. PLANT: often somewhat prostrate, 6–12" (15–30 cm) tall; leaves alternate, pinnately divided into 5 to 11 oblong lobes, margin coarsely toothed, green; seed pods narrow, ⁵⁄₁₆–½" (8–13 mm) long, long-stalked. HABITAT: waste areas, edges of lakes and rivers.

LEAVES OPPOSITE OR WHORLED, SIMPLE

Yellow Bedstraw
- *Galium verum* L.
- Madder family **Rubiaceae**

FLOWERING SEASON: June-July. FLOWERS: yellow, many, in densely flowered terminal and axial clusters, tiny, corolla with 4 sharply pointed, petal-like lobes. PLANT: 6–30" (15–75 cm) tall; leaves in whorls of 6 to 8, simple, very narrow, margin entire, green. HABITAT: fields and waste areas.

FLOWERS SYMMETRICAL, WITH 5 PETALS OR PETAL-LIKE PARTS

LEAVES BASAL, SIMPLE

Marsh Marigold, American Cowslip
- *Caltha palustris* L.
- Crowfoot family **Ranunculaceae**

FLOWERING SEASON: late April through May. FLOWERS: yellow, several, in a showy terminal cluster, about 1¼" (3.1 cm) wide, with 5 large, rounded, petal-like sepals. PLANT: 1–2' (30–60 cm) tall; leaves mostly basal, simple, heart- to kidney-shaped with a broadly rounded tip, margin entire to slightly scalloped, green. HABITAT: swamps and wet meadows.

LEAVES BASAL, COMPOUND

Barren Strawberry, False Strawberry
- *Waldsteinia fragarioides* (Michx.) Tratt.
- Rose family **Rosaceae**

FLOWERING SEASON: late April through May. FLOWERS: yellow, several in a loose terminal cluster, about ⁵⁄₁₆" (8 mm) wide, with 5 rounded petals. PLANT: creeping, 3–7" (7.5–17.5 cm) tall; leaves alternate or mostly basal, compound with 3 leaflets; leaflets obovate, margins toothed,

Black Mustard / *Brassica nigra*

Yellow Bedstraw / *Galium verum*

Celandine / *Chelidonium majus*

Creeping Yellow-cress / *Rorippa sylvestris*

Barren Strawberry, False Strawberry / *Waldsteinia fragarioides*

Marsh Marigold, American Cowslip / *Caltha palustris*

green. HABITAT: woodlands and shaded hillsides.

Mountain Avens
- *Geum peckii* Pursh
- Rose family **Rosaceae**

FLOWERING SEASON: June-August. FLOWERS: yellow, solitary to several in a loose terminal cluster, about 1" (2.5 cm) wide, with five notched petals. PLANT: 6–24" (15.5–60 cm) tall; leaves basal, alternate; basal leaves pinnately compound, terminal leaflet disproportionately large; alternate leaves much smaller; margins raggedly toothed, green. HABITAT: alpine areas. COMMENTS: *endangered. Do not disturb.* Known only from the White Mountains of New Hampshire and one location in Nova Scotia.

LEAVES ALTERNATE, SIMPLE

Purslane
- *Portulaca oleracea* L.
- Purslane family **Portulacaceae**

FLOWERING SEASON: July-September. FLOWERS: yellow, several, individual flowers found in the center of axial leaf clusters, up to ¼" (6 mm) wide, with 5 broad petals. PLANT: prostrate; leaves alternate or clustered at the end of 4–10" (10–25 cm) long purple stems, simple, obovate, thick and fleshy, margin entire, green. HABITAT: fields and waste areas.

Velvet-leaf
- *Abutilon theophrasti* Medic.
- Mallow family **Malvaceae**

FLOWERING SEASON: mid-August to late September. FLOWERS: yellow to orange-yellow, 1 to 3 in the upper axils; about 3–4" (1.9 cm) wide, with 5 rounded petals. PLANT: about 3–6' (0.9–1.8 m) tall; leaves alternate, simple, heart-shaped, large, margin entire, green. HABITAT: waste areas and fields, especially with recently disturbed soil.

COMMENTS: a nuisance plant of farmers' fields.

Mossy Stonecrop
- *Sedum acre* L.
- Sedum family **Crassulaceae**

FLOWERING SEASON: mid-June to mid-July. FLOWERS: bright yellow, several scattered along spreading stems, about ⅜" (9 mm) wide, with 4 to 5 lance-shaped petals. PLANT: creeping and spreading, 1–3" (2.5–7.5 cm) tall; leaves alternate, simple, ovate and appearing scale-like, thick and fleshy, margin entire, light green. HABITAT: on rocks and rocky soil, often wet areas.

Wild Black Currant
- *Ribes americanum* Mill.
- Currant family **Grossulariaceae**

FLOWERING SEASON: May. FLOWERS: greenish yellow, many, in drooping axial clusters of about 10, about 5/16" (8 mm) long, with 5 petals. PLANT: shrub, 3–4' (0.9–1.2 m) tall; leaves alternate and often clustered, simple, broadly maple-like with 3 to 5 lobes, margins toothed, green; fruit a drooping cluster of smooth ¼" (6 mm) black berries. HABITAT: moist woodlands and swamps. COMMENTS: wild gooseberry, *Ribes cynos-bati*, is a similar woodland shrub with bell-shaped flowers in clusters of 1 to 3 and 5/16–½" (8–13 mm) prickle-skinned fruit.

Butterfly-weed
- *Asclepias tuberosa* L.
- Milkweed family **Asclepiadaceae**

FLOWERING SEASON: mid-July through August. FLOWERS: orange, many in rounded terminal clusters, about ¼" (6 mm) wide, with 5 deeply recurved petals and a 5-pointed crown-like center. PLANT: 1–2' (30–60 cm) tall; leaves alternate, simple, narrowly oblong, margin entire, green. HABITAT: dry, often sandy soils.

Mountain Avens / *Geum peckii*

Purslane / *Portulaca oleracea*

Velvet-leaf / *Abutilon theophrasti*

Mossy Stonecrop / *Sedum acre*

Wild Black Currant / *Ribes americanum*

Butterfly-weed / *Asclepias tuberosa*

Clammy Ground-cherry
• *Physalis heterophylla* Nees
• Nightshade family **Solanaceae**
FLOWERING SEASON: July-September.
FLOWERS: greenish yellow to yellowish with a brownish to purplish center, several, scattered throughout the plant in axils; about ¾" (2 cm) wide, corolla broadly bell-shaped with 5 petal-like lobes, nodding. PLANT: about 1½–3' (45–90 cm) tall; leaves alternate along hairy branching stems, simple, obovate to broadly heart-shaped, margin toothed, green; fruit an edible spherical berry surrounded by a papery lantern-like husk. HABITAT: roadsides, waste areas, and previously cultivated fields. COMMENTS: numerous look-alike species occur.

Mullein, Velvet Dock, Devil's Tobacco
• *Verbascum thapsus* L.
• Figwort family **Scrophulariaceae**
FLOWERING SEASON: late May to September. FLOWERS: yellow, several to many in an elongated, sometimes branched terminal cluster, up to 1" (2.5 cm) wide, tubular at the base with 5 rounded petal-like lobes. PLANT: 2–7' (0.6–2.1 m) tall; leaves alternate, simple, oblong, densely pubescent, margin inconspicuously toothed, pale green. HABITAT: fields and waste areas.

LEAVES ALTERNATE, COMPOUND OR DEEPLY DIVIDED

Swamp Buttercup
• *Ranunculus hispidus* Michx.
• Crowfoot family **Ranunculaceae**
FLOWERING SEASON: late April to late May. FLOWERS: bright yellow, several, terminal, 1" (2.5 cm) or more wide, with 5 ovate petals. PLANT: 1–3' (30–90 cm) tall; leaves alternate, divided into 3 segments, leaflets distinctly stalked, margins sharply and unevenly toothed, green. HABITAT: swamps and moist low ground.

Creeping Buttercup
• *Ranunculus repens* L.
• Crowfoot family **Ranunculaceae**
FLOWERING SEASON: May-June. FLOWERS: bright yellow, several, terminal, nearly 1" (2.5 cm) wide, with 5 ovate petals. PLANT: creeping, usually less than 1' (30 cm) tall; leaves alternate, divided into 3 segments, terminal segment stalked, lateral segments stalkless, margins unevenly toothed, green with greenish white blotches. HABITAT: fields, roadsides, and waste areas.

Agrimony
• *Agrimonia striata* Michx.
• Rose family **Rosaceae**
FLOWERING SEASON: August into September. FLOWERS: yellow, several to many in slender (usually terminal) clusters, about ³⁄₁₆" (5 mm) wide, with 5 rounded petals. PLANT: 1–5' (0.3–1.5 m) tall; leaves alternate, pinnately compound typically with 5 large leaflets and smaller ones in between; large leaflets oblong to obovate, coarsely toothed, green; smaller leaflets lance-shaped, margins entire, green. HABITAT: dry woodlands.

Common Cinquefoil
• *Potentilla simplex* Michx.
• Rose family **Rosaceae**
FLOWERING SEASON: July. FLOWERS: yellow, few, terminal or in axils, ¼–½" (6–13 mm) wide, with 5 rounded petals. PLANT: trailing, stem 3–24" (7.5–60 cm) long; leaves alternate, palmately compound with 5 leaflets; leaflets oblong to lance-shaped, margins toothed, green; stem hairy. HABITAT: fields, waste areas, and open woods.

Clammy Ground-cherry / *Physalis heterophylla*

Agrimony / *Agrimonia striata*

Mullein, Velvet Dock, Devil's Tobacco / *Verbascum thapsus*

Creeping Buttercup / *Ranunculus repens*

Swamp Buttercup / *Ranunculus hispidus*

Common Cinquefoil / *Potentilla simplex*

Sulfur Cinquefoil, Five-fingers
• *Potentilla recta* L.
• Rose family **Rosaceae**
FLOWERING SEASON: mid-June to mid-August. FLOWERS: sulphur-yellow with an orange center, several to many in a loose terminal cluster, ½–¾" (1.3–1.9 cm) wide, with 5 notched petals. PLANT: 1–2' (30–60 cm) tall; leaves alternate, palmately divided with 5 to 7 lobes; margin coarsely toothed, somewhat pubescent, green; stem hairy. HABITAT: fields and waste areas.

Rough Cinquefoil
• *Potentilla norvegica* L.
• Rose family **Rosaceae**
FLOWERING SEASON: July. FLOWERS: yellow, several, terminal, up to ½" (1.3 cm) wide, with 5 rounded petals. PLANT: 6–30" (15–75 cm) tall; leaves alternate, 3-lobed, leaflets ovate to lance-shaped, margins toothed, green; stem roughened with short, stiff hairs. HABITAT: cultivated fields, waste areas, and roadsides.

Shrubby Cinquefoil
• *Potentilla fruticosa* L.
• Rose family **Rosaceae**
FLOWERING SEASON: late June through July. FLOWERS: bright yellow, solitary to several, terminal, ¾–1¼" (1.9–3.1 cm) wide, with 5 rounded petals. PLANT: shrub, 6–48" (15–120 cm) tall; leaves alternate, pinnately compound with 5 to 7 leaflets; leaflets oblong to lance-shaped, silky-pubescent, margins entire or slightly toothed, green. HABITAT: swamps and moist rocky places.

Yellow Wood-sorrel, Sour Grass
• *Oxalis stricta* L.
• Oxalis family **Oxalidaceae**
FLOWERING SEASON: mid-May through August. FLOWERS: yellow, solitary to several in leaf axils, about ½" (1.3 cm) wide, with 5 nearly round petals. PLANT: 4–12" (10–30 cm) tall; leaves alternate, compound with 3 leaflets; leaflets heart-shaped, margins entire, green, sour-tasting. HABITAT: roadsides, waste areas, fields, and open woodlands.

Wild Parsnip
• *Pastinaca sativa* L.
• Carrot family **Apiaceae**
FLOWERING SEASON: mid-June to mid-July. FLOWERS: yellow, many, in rounded, flat-topped terminal clusters 2–6" (5–15 cm) wide; individual flowers tiny, with 5 petals. PLANT: 2–5' (0.6–1.5 m) tall; leaves alternate, pinnately compound; leaflets ovate, lobed, margin toothed, green. HABITAT: roadsides, fields, and waste areas.

Golden Alexanders
• *Zizia aurea* (L.) Koch
• Carrot family **Apiaceae**
FLOWERING SEASON: mid May to mid June. FLOWERS: yellow, many in a flat-topped terminal cluster about 2½" (6 cm) wide; individual flowers tiny, with 5 petals. PLANT: 1–2½' (30–76 cm) tall; leaves alternate, compound with 3 divisions containing up to 9 leaflets; leaflets ovate to somewhat lance-shaped, margins toothed, green. HABITAT: moist meadows, roadsides, swamps, and edges of open woodlands.

Sulfur Cinquefoil, Five-fingers / *Potentilla recta*

Rough Cinquefoil / *Potentilla norvegica*

Shrubby Cinquefoil / *Potentilla fruticosa*

Yellow Wood-sorrel, Sour Grass / *Oxalis stricta*

Wild Parsnip / *Pastinaca sativa*

Golden Alexanders / *Zizia aurea*

LEAVES OPPOSITE OR WHORLED, SIMPLE

Canadian St. John's-wort
•*Hypericum canadense* L.
•Mangosteen family **Clusiaceae**
FLOWERING SEASON: July-August. FLOW-ERS: yellow, several, in loosely flowered terminal clusters, about ¼" (6 mm) wide, with 5 rounded petals. PLANT: 6–20" (15–50 cm) tall; leaves opposite, simple, very narrow, margin entire, green. HABITAT: wet, sandy soil.

St. John's-wort
•*Hypericum perforatum* L.
•Mangosteen family **Clusiaceae**
FLOWERING SEASON: August. FLOWERS: yellow, several to many in terminal clusters, up to 1" (2.5 cm) wide, with 5 rounded petals with tiny black dots along the margin. PLANT: 1–2' (30–61 cm) tall; leaves opposite, simple, oblong, margin entire, green. HABITAT: fields, roadsides, and waste areas. COMMENTS: there are many species of yellow St. John's-worts in this region. Marsh St. John's-wort, *Triadenum virginicum,* has pinkish flowers in small terminal and axial clusters and is common in fens.

Swamp-candles
•*Lysimachia terrestris* (L.) BSP.
•Primrose family **Primulaceae**
FLOWERING SEASON: late June through July. FLOWERS: yellow with purple markings surrounding the center, many in a tall, slender terminal cluster, about ⅜" (9 mm) wide with 5 narrow petal-like lobes. PLANT: 8–24" (20–60 cm) tall; leaves mostly opposite, simple, lance-shaped, margin entire, green. HABITAT: swamps and moist areas.

Fringed Loosestrife
•*Lysimachia ciliata* L.
•Primrose family **Primulaceae**
FLOWERING SEASON: mid-July to mid-August. FLOWERS: yellow, several, in small axial groups, about ¾" (1.9 cm) wide, with 5 rounded, fringed-tipped, petal-like lobes. PLANT: 1–4' (0.3–1.2 m) tall; leaves opposite or whorled, simple, broadly lance-shaped, margin entire, green. HABITAT: moist meadows and thickets.

Moneywort, Creeping-Charlie
•*Lysimachia nummularia* L.
•Primrose family **Primulaceae**
FLOWERING SEASON: mid-June to mid-July. FLOWERS: yellow, several, in axial pairs, up to 1" (2.5 cm) wide, with 5 rounded, petal-like lobes. PLANT: prostrate with stems up to 2' (60 cm) long; leaves opposite, simple, nearly round, margin entire, green. HABITAT: moist fields and open woodlands.

Garden Loosestrife, Golden-cups
•*Lysimachia punctata* L.
•Primrose family **Primulaceae**
FLOWERING SEASON: early June to early July. FLOWERS: yellow, many in crowded axial clusters, about ¾" (2 cm) wide, with 5 broad petal-like lobes. PLANT: about 2–3' (0.6–1 m) tall; leaves whorled or opposite, simple, broadly lance-shaped, margin entire, green. HABITAT: escaping from cultivation in waste areas and roadsides.

Canadian St. John's-wort / *Hypericum canadense*

St. John's-wort / *Hypericum perforatum*

Moneywort, Creeping-Charlie / *Lysimachia nummularia*

Garden Loosestrife, Golden-cups / *Lysimachia punctata*

Swamp-candles / *Lysimachia terrestris*

Fringed Loosestrife / *Lysimachia ciliata*

FLOWERS SYMMETRICAL, WITH 6 PETALS OR PETAL-LIKE PARTS

AQUATIC, LEAVES FLOATING OR JUST ABOVE WATER

Yellow Pond-lily, Spatterdock

•*Nuphar luteum* (L.) Sibth. and Smith
•Waterlily family **Nymphaeaceae**
FLOWERING SEASON: mid-June through August. FLOWERS: yellow, solitary, terminal, 1½–3½" (3.8–8.8 cm) wide, with usually 6 oblong, petal-like sepals. PLANT: leaves up to 1' (30 cm) long, usually floating, simple, ovate with a deeply heart-shaped base, margin entire, green. HABITAT: aquatic, including ponds, lakes, and slowly moving streams. COMMENTS: some authorities now consider this a complex of several species.

LEAVES BASAL, SIMPLE

Lemon-lily, Yellow Daylily

•*Hemerocallis lilioasphodelus* L.
•Lily family **Liliaceae**
FLOWERING SEASON: mid-May through June. FLOWERS: yellow, several on a tall stem with only 1 to 3 blooming at a time, about 4" (10 cm) long, large and showy, trumpet-shaped, perianth with 6 flaring and somewhat recurved parts. PLANT: 3–4' (0.9–1.2 m) tall; leaves many, basal, simple, long and narrow, margin entire, green. HABITAT: fields, roadsides. COMMENTS: unlike the orange daylily, *Hemerocallis fulva*, the lemon lily produces seeds.

Orange Daylily

•*Hemerocallis fulva* (L.) L.
•Lily family **Liliaceae**
FLOWERING SEASON: mid-June through July. FLOWERS: orange, 6 to 15 on a tall stem with only 1 to 3 blooming at a time, about 4–5" (10–12.5 cm) long, large and showy, trumpet-shaped, perianth with 6 flaring and recurved parts. PLANT: 3–6'

(0.9–1.8 m) tall; leaves many, basal, simple, long and narrow, margin entire, green. HABITAT: fields, roadsides. COMMENTS: flowers last only one day, hence the common name daylily.

Troutlily, Dog-tooth Violet

•*Erythronium americanum* Ker
•Lily family **Liliaceae**
FLOWERING SEASON: late April to mid-May. FLOWER: yellow, solitary, terminal, about 1¼" (3.1 cm) long, perianth with 6 lance-shaped spreading to somewhat recurved parts. PLANT: 6–12" (15–30 cm) tall; leaves 2, basal, simple, lance-shaped, margin entire, fleshy, green, often with purplish or brownish mottling. HABITAT: woodlands.

Clintonia, Woodlily

•*Clintonia borealis* (Ait.) Raf.
•Lily family **Liliaceae**
FLOWERING SEASON: late May through June. FLOWERS: yellow to greenish yellow, 3 to 6 in a terminal cluster, about ¾" (1.9 cm) long, perianth with 6 long, narrow, petal-like parts, usually drooping. PLANT: 6–15" (15–37.5 cm) tall; leaves usually 3, basal, simple, oval, margin entire, green. HABITAT: woodlands.

LEAVES ALTERNATE, SIMPLE

Tiger Lily

•*Lilium lancifolium* Thunb.
•Lily family **Liliaceae**
FLOWERING SEASON: mid-July to mid-August. FLOWERS: orange-red, conspicuously purple-spotted inside, 5 to 25 flowers in a terminal cluster, about 3¼" (8.1 cm) wide, perianth with 6 large, spreading, and deeply recurved petal-like parts, stamens fully protruding, nodding. PLANT: 2–5' (0.6–1.5 m) tall; leaves alternate, simple, lance-shaped, margin entire, green; blackish bulblets in the upper axils. HABITAT: fields, hedgerows, and roadsides.

Yellow Pond-lily, Spatterdock / *Nuphar luteum*

Lemon-lily, Yellow Daylily / *Hemerocallis lilioasphodelus*

Orange Daylily / *Hemerocallis fulva*

Clintonia, Woodlily / *Clintonia borealis*

Troutlily, Dog-tooth Violet / *Erythronium americanum*

Tiger Lily / *Lilium lancifolium*

Wild-oats
•*Uvularia sessilifolia* L.
•Lily family **Liliaceae**
FLOWERING SEASON: mid to late May.
FLOWER: greenish yellow, solitary, axial,
about 1" (2.5 cm) long, perianth with 6
long, narrow, petal-like parts, nodding.
PLANT: 10–12" (25–30 cm) tall; leaves
alternate along a forking stem, simple,
lance-shaped, margin entire, green.
HABITAT: woodlands.

Bellwort
•*Uvularia grandiflora* Sm.
•Lily family **Liliaceae**
FLOWERING SEASON: mid-April to mid-
May. FLOWER: yellow, usually solitary
and terminal, about 1¼" (3.1 cm) long,
perianth with 6 long, narrow, petal-like
parts, smooth or slightly granular
within, nodding. PLANT: 6–20" (15–
50 cm) tall; leaves alternate on a forking
stem, simple, oblong to oval, penetra-
ted by the stem, margin entire, lower surface pubescent during flowering season,
green. HABITAT: woodlands.

LEAVES OPPOSITE OR WHORLED, SIMPLE

Common Barberry
•*Berberis vulgaris* L.
•Barberry family **Berberidaceae**
FLOWERING SEASON: mid-May to mid-
June. FLOWERS: yellow, several to many
in pendant, slender axial clusters, about
⁵⁄₁₆" (8 mm) wide, with 6 rounded petals.
PLANT: shrub, 6–8' (1.8–2.4 m) tall;
leaves opposite or whorled, simple,
paddle-shaped, margin sharply toothed,
green. HABITAT: thickets, pastures, and
hedgerows. COMMENTS: the scarlet
oblong berries are pleasantly acidic.

Indian Cucumber-root
•*Medeola virginiana* L.
•Lily family **Liliaceae**
FLOWERING SEASON: June to early July.
FLOWERS: greenish yellow, 2 to 9 in a
drooping terminal cluster, about ¾"
(2 cm) wide, perianth with 6 petal-like
parts. PLANT: 1–2½' (30–75 cm) tall;
leaves in 2 whorls; leaves of lower whorl
large and about 6 in number, leaves of
upper whorl smaller, fewer, terminal;
simple, lance-shaped, margin entire,
green. HABITAT: woodlands.

Woodlily
•*Lilium philadelphicum* L.
•Lily family **Liliaceae**
FLOWERING SEASON: late June to early
July. FLOWER: reddish orange, purple-
spotted inside, usually solitary or sometimes 2, terminal, about 3½" (8.8 cm)
wide, perianth with 6 spreading, petal-
like parts, flower facing upwards. PLANT:
1–3' (30–90 cm) tall; leaves whorled,
simple, lance-shaped, margin entire,
green. HABITAT: woods and thickets

Canada Lily
•*Lilium canadense* L.
•Lily family **Liliaceae**
FLOWERING SEASON: late June to mid-
July. FLOWERS: yellow, occasionally red,
with numerous spots inside, 1 to 16 in
showy terminal clusters, about 3¾"
(9.4 cm) wide, perianth with 6 large,
spreading, and somewhat recurved petal-
like parts, thickened tips of stamens protruding from flowers, nodding. PLANT:
2–5' (0.6–1.5 m) tall; leaves whorled,
simple, lance-shaped, margin entire,
green. HABITAT: swamps, moist meadows, and fields.

Bellwort / *Uvularia grandiflora*

Wild-oats / *Uvularia sessilifolia*

Common Barberry / *Berberis vulgaris*

Indian Cucumber-root / *Medeola virginiana*

Woodlily / *Lilium philadelphicum*

Canada Lily / *Lilium canadense*

Turk's-cap Lily

•*Lilium superbum* L.

•Lily family **Liliaceae**

FLOWERING SEASON: July.   FLOWERS: orange, orange-yellow or occasionally red, purple-spotted inside, 3 to 40, in showy terminal clusters, about 3" (7.5 cm) wide, perianth with 6 large, spreading, and deeply recurved petal-like parts, nearly all of the stamens protruding from flowers, nodding. PLANT: 3–8' (0.9–2.4 m) tall; leaves whorled, simple, lance-shaped, margin entire, green. HABITAT: meadows and open moist areas.

FLOWERS SYMMETRICAL, WITH 7 OR MORE PETALS OR PETAL-LIKE PARTS

LEAVES BASAL, SIMPLE

Dandelion

•*Taraxacum officinale* Weber ex Wiggers

•Aster family **Asteraceae**

FLOWERING SEASON: late April to early June; a few into fall. FLOWERHEADS: yellow, 1 to few on terminal stalks, individual flowerheads about 1½" (3.8 cm) wide, rimmed with many oblong, minutely 5-toothed, petal-like rays. PLANT: 2–18" (5–45 cm) tall; leaves basal, simple, oblong to paddle-shaped, margin unevenly and coarsely toothed, green. HABITAT: fields, lawns, and waste areas.

Cat's Ear

•*Hypochaeris radicata* L.

•Aster family **Asteraceae**

FLOWERING SEASON: mid-July to September. FLOWERHEADS: yellow, several in small terminal clusters, individual flowerheads about 1" (2.5 cm) wide, rimmed with many rectangular minutely 5-toothed petal-like rays. PLANT: 1–2' (30–61 cm) tall; leaves basal, simple, oblong to paddle-shaped, margin unevenly and coarsely toothed, pubescent, green. HABITAT: waste areas and fields.

Coltsfoot

•*Tussilago farfara* L.

•Aster family **Asteraceae**

FLOWERING SEASON: April-May. FLOWERHEADS: yellow, few, each terminal on an individual scaly 3–18" (7.5–45 cm) tall stem, individual flowerheads about 1" (2.5 cm) wide, rimmed with many narrow, petal-like rays, blooming before the leaves emerge. LEAVES: basal, simple, nearly round with very shallow angularly-sided lobes, margin toothed, green, pubescent underneath. HABITAT: moist soil, meadows, and roadsides.

Orange Hawkweed, Devil's Paint-brush

•*Hieracium aurantiacum* L.

•Aster family **Asteraceae**

FLOWERING SEASON: June-July. FLOWERHEADS: orange to reddish orange, few to several in a loose terminal cluster, individual flowerheads up to 1" (2.5 cm) wide, rimmed with 2 to 3 layers of rectangular, minutely 5-toothed, petal-like rays. PLANT: 6–20" (15–50 cm) tall; leaves basal, simple, spathulate, pubescent, margin entire, green. HABITAT: fields, roadsides, and woodland openings. COMMENTS: although there are several yellow-flowerhead hawkweeds, this is the only species with orange flowers.

LEAVES ALTERNATE, SIMPLE

Elecampane

•*Inula helenium* L.

•Aster family **Asteraceae**

FLOWERING SEASON: mid-July to mid-August. FLOWERHEADS: yellow, several,

Turk's-cap Lily / *Lilium superbum*

Orange Hawkweed, Devil's Paint-brush / *Hieracium aurantiacum*

Coltsfoot / *Tussilago farfara*

Dandelion / *Taraxacum officinale*

Cat's Ear / *Hypochaeris radicata*

Elecampane / *Inula helenium*

terminal; individual flowerheads 2–4" (5–10 cm) wide, rimmed with many very narrow, minutely 3-toothed, petal-like rays. PLANT: 2–6' (0.6–1.8 m) tall; leaves alternate and basal, simple, broadly lance-shaped, rough textured, margin toothed, green. HABITAT: moist meadows.

Yellow Goat's-beard

• *Tragopogon pratensis* L.
• Aster family **Asteraceae**

FLOWERING SEASON: mid-May to late June. FLOWERHEAD: yellow, solitary, terminal, 1½–2½" (3.8–6.3 cm) wide, rimmed with many oblong, minutely 5-toothed, petal-like rays. PLANT: 15–36" (37.5–90 cm) tall; leaves basal and alternate, simple, long and narrow, margin entire, green. HABITAT: fields and waste areas. COMMENTS: salsify, *Tragopogon porrifolius*, is a very similar plant with purplish flowerheads.

Alpine Goldenrod, Northern Goldenrod

• *Solidago cutleri* Fernald
• Aster family **Asteraceae**

FLOWERING SEASON: August-September. FLOWERHEADS: yellow, few to several in a somewhat dense terminal cluster, individual flowerheads about ⁵⁄₁₆" (8 mm) high, rimmed with several tiny, petal-like rays. PLANT: 3–12" (7.5–30 cm) tall; leaves alternate, simple, of 2 types; basal and lower leaves obovate to spathulate with prominent stems; upper leaves narrower, lacking stems; margin toothed on lower leaves, green. HABITAT: alpine summits.

Black-eyed Susan

• *Rudbeckia hirta* L.
• Aster family **Asteraceae**

FLOWERING SEASON: July-August. FLOWERHEADS: orangish yellow with a raised purplish brown center, solitary to few,

terminal, individual flowerheads 2–4" (5–10 cm) wide, rimmed with 10 to 20 somewhat oblong, notch-tipped, petal-like rays. PLANT: 1–3' (30–91 cm) tall; leaves alternate, simple, lance-shaped, margin entire to slightly toothed, green. HABITAT: fields and meadows.

Sneezeweed

• *Helenium autumnale* L.
• Aster family **Asteraceae**

FLOWERING SEASON: late August through September. FLOWERHEADS: yellow with a raised yellow globular center, several to many, terminal, individual flowerheads 1–2" (2.5–5 cm) wide, rimmed with 10 to 18 drooping, wedge-shaped, 3-lobed, petal-like rays. PLANT: 2–6' (0.6–1.8 m) tall; leaves alternate, simple, lance-shaped, margin toothed, green. HABITAT: swamps and wet meadows. COMMENTS: *Helenium flexosum*, also known as sneezeweed, is a very similar plant with a raised brownish center.

LEAVES ALTERNATE, COMPOUND OR DEEPLY LOBED OR DIVIDED

Green-headed Coneflower

• *Rudbeckia laciniata* L.
• Aster family **Asteraceae**

FLOWERING SEASON: late July to early September. FLOWERHEADS: yellow with a raised, ovoid greenish-yellow center, several, terminal, individual flowerheads 2½–4" (6.3–10 cm) wide, rimmed with 6 to 10 drooping, somewhat oblong, petal-like rays. PLANT: 3–10' (0.9–3 m) tall; leaves alternate, simple, with 3 to 7 deeply cleft pinnate lobes, margin large-toothed, green. HABITAT: moist thickets.

Yellow Goat's-beard / *Tragopogon pratensis*

Black-eyed Susan / *Rudbeckia hirta*

Alpine Goldenrod, Northern Goldenrod / *Solidago cutleri*

Green-headed Coneflower / *Rudbeckia laciniata*

Sneezeweed / *Helenium autumnale*

Golden Ragwort
•*Senecio aureus* L.
•Aster family **Asteraceae**
FLOWERING SEASON: May-June. FLOWER-
HEADS: golden yellow, several to many in
terminal clusters, individual flowerheads
⅝–¾" (1.6–2 cm) wide, rimmed with
8–12 minutely toothed petal-like rays
surrounding a yellow center. PLANT:
1–2½' (30–76 cm) tall; leaves of two
types; basal leaves heart-shaped, simple,
with long stalks; upper leaves alternate,
deeply lobed, clasping; margin toothed,
green. HABITAT: swamps, wet meadows,
and wet woodlands.

LEAVES ALTERNATE OR OPPOSITE, OFTEN BOTH ON THE SAME PLANT

Thin-leaf Sunflower
•*Helianthus decapetalus* L.
•Aster family **Asteraceae**
FLOWERING SEASON: August-September.
FLOWERHEADS: yellow, several, terminal,
individual flowerheads about 2½"
(6.3 cm) wide, with 8 to 15 somewhat
oblong, petal-like rays. PLANT: 1–5'
(0.3–1.5 m) tall; leaves opposite or alternate, simple, broadly lance-shaped with
a pointed tip, margin toothed, green.
HABITAT: moist woodlands. COMMENTS:
a very common woodland sunflower.

Giant Sunflower
•*Helianthus giganteus* L.
•Aster family **Asteraceae**
FLOWERING SEASON:September-October.
FLOWERHEADS: yellow, several, terminal,
individual flowerheads about 2½"
(6.3 cm) or more wide, rimmed with 10
to 20 or more lance-shaped, petal-like
rays. PLANT: 3–12' (0.9–3.6 m) tall;
leaves opposite and alternate on a rough
stem, simple, lance-shaped, margin
toothed, green. HABITAT: swamps and
wet meadows.

Jerusalem Artichoke
•*Helianthus tuberosus* L.
•Aster family **Asteraceae**
FLOWERING SEASON: September through
mid-October. FLOWERHEADS: yellow,
several, terminal, individual flowerheads
about 3" (7.5 cm) wide, rimmed with 12
to 20 oblong, petal-like rays. PLANT:
6–12' (1.8–3.6 m) tall; leaves opposite
and alternate on a rough stem, simple,
ovate tapering to a pointed tip, margin
toothed, green. HABITAT: creek and river
banks and open moist soil. COMMENTS:
prized for its edible, somewhat potato-
like tuber.

LEAVES OPPOSITE, SIMPLE

Bur-marigold, Stick-tights
•*Bidens cernua* L.
•Aster family **Asteraceae**
FLOWERING SEASON: September. FLOW-
ERHEADS: yellow, several to many,
terminal and upper axial, individual
flowerheads ½–1" (1.3–2.5 cm) wide,
rimmed with 6 to 10 short, petal-like
rays. PLANT: 1–3' (30–90 cm) tall;
leaves opposite, simple, narrowly lance-
shaped, margin toothed, green. HABITAT:
wet soil.

Jerusalem Artichoke / *Helianthus tuberosus*

Golden Ragwort / *Senecio aureus*

Thin-leaf Sunflower / *Helianthus decapetalus*

Giant Sunflower / *Helianthus giganteus*

Bur-marigold, Stick-tights / *Bidens cernua*

FLOWERS NOT RADIALLY SYMMETRICAL; FLOWERS MINUTE, FILAMENTOUS, TUBULAR WITH NO PETAL-LIKE LOBES, OR WITH NO OBVIOUS PETAL-LIKE PARTS

LACKING TYPICAL LEAVES

Squawroot
•*Conopholis americana* (L.) Wallr.
•Broom-rape family **Orobanchaceae**
FLOWERING SEASON: June-July. **FLOW-ERS:** pale yellow, many completely cover-ing a thick, cone-like stem, about ½" (1.3 cm) long, tubular and 2-lipped; upper lip erect and hood-like; lower lip 3-lobed. **PLANT:** 3–10" (7.5–25 cm) tall; leaves absent, stem covered with large, straw-colored, lance-shaped scales. **HABITAT:** woodlands. **COMMENTS:** para-sitic on tree roots.

Beechdrops
•*Epifagus virginiana* (L.) Bartr.
•Broom-rape family **Orobanchaceae**
FLOWERING SEASON: late August to early October. **FLOWERS:** yellowish with pur-plish brown stripes, many, alternate along branching stems; about ⁵⁄₁₆" (8 mm) long, tubular with 4 tiny tri-angular lobes. **PLANT:** 6–24" (15–60 cm) tall; leaves absent; stem yellowish brown. **HABITAT:** beech woodlands. **COMMENTS:** parasitic on beech tree roots.

AQUATIC

Horned Bladderwort
•*Utricularia cornuta* Michx.
•Bladderwort family **Lentibulariaceae**
FLOWERING SEASON: August. **FLOWERS:** yellow, 1 to 6, usually paired, terminal, about ¾" (1.9 cm) long, tubular and 2-lipped; upper lip small and erect; lower lip helmet-shaped with a conspicuous spur at the base. **PLANT:** aquatic, 3–10" (7.5–25 cm) tall; leaves submerged along an underwater stem, filamentous with small globular bladders. **HABITAT:** edges

of ponds, fens, and other bodies of water. **COMMENTS:** the leaf bladders function to trap minute aquatic animals for food. Several other yellow bladderwort species also occur in this region.

LEAVES ALTERNATE, SIMPLE

Yellow Violet
•*Viola pubescens* Ait.
•Violet family **Violaceae**
FLOWERING SEASON: May. **FLOWERS:** yel-low with purple veining, few, terminal, up to ¾" (1.9 cm) wide, with 5 unequal rounded petals. **PLANT:** 5–20" (12.5–50 cm) tall; leaves basal and alternate, simple, broadly heart-shaped, margin toothed, green. **HABITAT:** woodlands.

Leatherwood
•*Dirca palustris* L.
•Mezereum family **Thymeleaceae**
FLOWERING SEASON: late April to mid-May. **FLOWERS:** yellowish, many in axial clusters of 2–4 but usually 3, about ¼" (6 mm) long, tubular with 4 very shallow lobes. **PLANT:** shrub, 2–6' (0.6–1.8 m) tall; leaves alternate, simple, oval, margin entire, green. **HABITAT:** moist woodlands.

Cypress Spurge
•*Euphorbia cyparissias* L.
•Spurge family **Euphorbiaceae**
FLOWERING SEASON: mid-May to mid-June. **FLOWERS:** yellowish green, becom-ing reddish orange in age, many in about 2½" (6.5 cm) wide terminal or smaller axial flat-topped clusters; individual flowers minute, in small clusters above 2 showy, petal-like bracts. **PLANT:** up to 1' (30 cm) tall; leaves whorled (just below the flowers) or alternate, simple, long

Cypress Spurge / *Euphorbia cyparissias*

Beechdrops / *Epifagus virginiana*

Yellow Violet / *Viola pubescens*

Squawroot / *Conopholis americana*

Horned Bladderwort / *Utricularia cornuta*

Leatherwood / *Dirca palustris*

and narrow, margin entire, green. HABITAT: roadsides and waste areas. COMMENTS: the milky sap of this and other spurges is *poisonous.*

Spotted Jewelweed, Touch-me-not
• *Impatiens capensis* Meerb.
• Touch-me-not family **Balsaminaceae**
FLOWERING SEASON: mid-July to early September. FLOWERS: orange-yellow mottled with reddish brown, solitary to several in leaf axils, ¾–1" (1.9–2.5 cm) long, tubular with a prominent curved basal spur and showy frontal lobes. PLANT: 2–5' (0.6–1.5 m) tall; leaves alternate, simple, ovate to elliptic, margin toothed, green. HABITAT: moist soil.

Pale Jewelweed, Touch-me-not
• *Impatiens pallida* Nutt.
• Touch-me-not family **Balsaminaceae**
FLOWERING SEASON: July-August. FLOWERS: pale yellow to yellow, sparingly mottled with reddish brown dots or dotless, solitary to several in leaf axils, 1–1¼" (2.5–3.1 cm) long, tubular with a prominent curved basal spur and showy frontal lobes. PLANT: 2–5' (0.6–1.5 m) tall; leaves alternate, simple, ovate to elliptic, margin toothed, green. HABITAT: moist soil.

Butter-and-eggs
• *Linaria vulgaris* Mill.
• Figwort family **Scrophulariaceae**
FLOWERING SEASON: mid-June through August. FLOWERS: pale yellow with orange on a portion of the lower lip, several in a narrow densely flowered terminal cluster, about 1–1¼ (2.5–3.1 cm) long, tubular with 2 lips and a long basal spur. PLANT: 1–2' (30–60 cm) tall; leaves alternate, simple, long and narrow, margin entire, green. HABITAT: fields, roadsides, and waste areas.

Wood-betony, Lousewort
• *Pedicularis canadensis* L.
• Figwort family **Scrophulariaceae**
FLOWERING SEASON: mid-May to early June. FLOWERS: bicolored, yellow and purplish brown, several in a dense terminal cluster, about ¾" (1.9 cm) long, tubular, 2-lipped; upper lip large and hood-shaped; lower lip 3-lobed. PLANT: 6–18" (15–45 cm) tall; leaves mostly alternate, simple, oblong and many-lobed, margin bluntly toothed, green. HABITAT: woodlands and along streams.

Blue-stem Goldenrod
• *Solidago caesia* L.
• Aster family **Asteraceae**
FLOWERING SEASON: September into October. FLOWERHEADS: yellow, many, in short axial clusters, individual flowerheads up to ¼" (6 mm) high, rimmed with 5 tiny petal-like rays. PLANT: 1–3' (30–90 cm) tall; leaves alternate on a bluish to purple stem, simple, lance-shaped, margin sharply toothed, green. HABITAT: woodlands and thickets.

Late Goldenrod
• *Solidago gigantea* Ait.
• Aster family **Asteraceae**
FLOWERING SEASON: August-September. FLOWERHEADS: yellow, many in a showy branching terminal cluster, individual flowerheads about ¼" (6 mm) high, rimmed with 7 to 15 tiny, petal-like rays. PLANT: 3–8' (0.9–2.4 m) tall; leaves alternate on a smooth stem, simple, lance-shaped, margin sharply toothed, green. HABITAT: open moist soil. COMMENTS: Canada goldenrod, *Solidago canadensis*, a very similar species of drier soils, has a pubescent stem and flowerheads about ⅛" (3 mm) high.

Butter-and-eggs / *Linaria vulgaris*

Wood-betony, Lousewort / *Pedicularis canadensis*

Pale Jewelweed, Touch-me-not / *Impatiens pallida*

Spotted Jewelweed, Touch-me-not / *Impatiens capensis*

Blue-stem Goldenrod / *Solidago caesia*

Late Goldenrod / *Solidago gigantea*

Yellow Lady's Slipper

- *Cypripedium parviflorum* Salisb.
- Orchid family **Orchidaceae**

FLOWERING SEASON: mid-May to mid-June. FLOWERS: lip yellow, sepals and petals from yellowish green (*var. pubescens*) to dark reddish brown (*var. parviflorum* and *makasin*), 1 to 2, terminal; lip about ¾–1¼" (1.9–3.1 cm) long in *var. parviflorum* and *makasin*, up to about 2" long (5 cm) in *var. pubescens*, pouch-like. PLANT: 1–2' (30–60 cm) tall; leaves 3 to 5, alternate, simple, lance-shaped to nearly round, margin entire, green. HABITAT: variable, from dry to more often moist woodlands, swamps, and wooded fens.

LEAVES ALTERNATE, COMPOUND OR DEEPLY DIVIDED

Early Meadow-rue

- *Thalictrum dioicum* L.
- Crowfoot family **Ranunculaceae**

FLOWERING SEASON: late April to mid-May. FLOWERS: greenish to yellowish, several to many in a terminal cluster, about ¼" (6 mm) long, composed of a tassel-like mass of yellowish thread-like stamens and about 5 tiny petal-like sepals. PLANT: 1–2' (30–60 cm) tall; leaves alternate, compound with numerous leaflets; leaflets rounded with 5 to 9 lobes, green. HABITAT: woodlands.

Black Medick

- *Medicago lupulina* L.
- Bean family **Fabaceae**

FLOWERING SEASON: June-August FLOWERS: yellow, many, in oblong ¼" (6 mm) tall flowerheads; individual flowers tiny. PLANT: often prostrate, up to 2' (60 cm) long; leaves alternate, compound with 3 leaflets; leaflets obovate, margins minutely toothed, green; fruit a cluster of black, tightly spiraled pods. HABITAT: fields,

lawns, and waste areas. COMMENTS: often found in stunted form in lawns.

Bird's-foot Trefoil

- *Lotus corniculata* L.
- Bean family **Fabaceae**

FLOWERING SEASON: late May into September. FLOWERS: yellow, many, 3 to 12 in rounded clusters scattered throughout the plant, about ⅝" (1.6 cm) long, pea-like. PLANT: trailing or ascending, 3–24" (7.5–60 cm) long; leaves alternate, compound with 3 leaflets; leaflets obovate, margins entire, green. HABITAT: meadows, roadsides, and waste areas. COMMENTS: seeds in several slender pods that resemble a bird's foot.

Yellow Sweet-clover

- *Melilotus altissima* Thuill.
- Bean family **Fabaceae**

FLOWERING SEASON: June-August. FLOWERS: yellow, many, in slender 2–4" (5–10 cm) long, often 1-sided axial clusters, about ¼" (6 mm) long, narrowly pea-like. PLANT: 3–5' (0.9–1.5 m) tall; leaves alternate, compound with 3 leaflets; leaflets narrowly oblong, margin toothed, green. HABITAT: fields, roadsides, and waste areas.

Pineapple-weed

- *Matricaria discoidea* DC.
- Aster family **Asteraceae**

FLOWERING SEASON: late May into August. FLOWERHEADS: greenish yellow, many, terminal and axial, individual flowerheads up to ⁵⁄₁₆" (8 mm) wide, appearing like a small daisy without petals. PLANT: 6–18" (15–45 cm) tall; leaves alternate, simple, pinnately divided into many narrow lobes, margin toothed, green, giving off a pineapple-like fragrance when torn. HABITAT: waste areas, meadows, and roadsides.

Early Meadow-rue / *Thalictrum dioicum*

Bird's-foot Trefoil / *Lotus corniculata*

Yellow Lady's Slipper / *Cypripedium parviflorum*

Yellow Sweet-clover / *Melilotus altissima*

Black Medick / *Medicago lupulina*

Pineapple-weed / *Matricaria discoidea*

LEAVES OPPOSITE, SIMPLE

Horse-balm
•*Collinsonia canadensis* L.
•Mint family **Lamiaceae**
FLOWERING SEASON: August. FLOWERS: light yellow, several to many in a loose terminal cluster, about ½" (1.3 cm) long, tubular with 2 lips; upper lip 3-lobed, lower lip 2-lobed, lemony fragrance. PLANT: 2–5' (0.6–1.5 m) tall; leaves opposite on a square stem, simple, ovate, margin coarsely and sharply toothed, green. HABITAT: moist woodlands.

Dotted Horsemint
•*Monarda punctata* L.
•Mint family **Lamiaceae**
FLOWERING SEASON: late July to early September. FLOWERS: yellowish with purple spots, many, in circular axillary or terminal clusters, about 1" (2.5 cm) long, tubular with 2 elongated lips; upper lip 2-lobed, lower lip 3-lobed. PLANT: 2–3' (60–90 cm) tall; leaves opposite on a square stem, simple, lance-shaped, margin toothed, green. HABITAT: sandy soils, frequently found along the ocean.

Rattlebox, Yellow Rattle
•*Rhinanthus crista-galli* L.
•Figwort family **Scrophulariaceae**
FLOWERING SEASON: late June to July. FLOWERS: yellow, several in a terminal, usually 1-sided cluster; ½–¾" (1.3–2 cm) long, tubular, 2-lipped; upper lip large and hood-shaped; lower lip 3-lobed. PLANT: 6–18" (15–46 cm) tall; leaves opposite, simple, broadly lance-shaped, margin coarsely toothed, green. HABITAT: meadows. COMMENTS: the base of the flower swells into a bladder-like capsule in which the seeds rattle when ripe.

Bush Honeysuckle
•*Diervilla lonicera* Mill.
•Honeysuckle family **Caprifoliaceae**
FLOWERING SEASON: June. FLOWERS: yellow, 1 to 5 in terminal clusters, about ¾" (1.9 cm) long, tubular with 5 recurved petal-like lobes. PLANT: shrub, 2–4' (0.6–1.2 m) tall; leaves opposite, simple, lance-shaped, margin minutely toothed, green. HABITAT: woodlands.

Early Fly Honeysuckle
•*Lonicera canadensis* Bartr.
•Honeysuckle family **Caprifoliaceae**
FLOWERING SEASON: May. FLOWERS: yellow to greenish yellow, in axial pairs, about ¾" (1.9 cm) long, funnel-shaped with 5 equal lobes. PLANT: shrub, 2–5' (0.6–1.5 m) tall; leaves opposite, simple, oval, margin entire, green. HABITAT: woodlands.

Tartarian Honeysuckle
•*Lonicera tartarica* L.
•Honeysuckle family **Caprifoliaceae**
FLOWERING SEASON: mid-May to mid-June. FLOWERS: pink to white or yellowish, many, in axial pairs, about ¾" (1.9 cm) long, tubular with 5 unequal, narrow, petal-like lobes. PLANT: shrub, 5–10' (1.5–3 m) tall; leaves opposite, simple, ovate, margin entire, green. HABITAT: hedgerows, thickets, and open woodlots.

Horse-balm / *Collinsonia canadensis*

Early Fly Honeysuckle / *Lonicera canadensis*

Rattlebox, Yellow Rattle / *Rhinanthus crista-galli*

Tartarian Honeysuckle / *Lonicera tartarica*

Dotted Horsemint / *Monarda punctata*

Bush Honeysuckle / *Diervilla lonicera*

PART FOUR

GREEN FLOWERS

&❧

FLOWERS SYMMETRICAL, WITH 5 PETALS OR PETAL-LIKE PARTS

LEAVES ALTERNATE, COMPOUND

Poison Ivy

- *Toxicodendron radicans* (L.) Kuntze
- Sumac family **Anacardiaceae**

FLOWERING SEASON: June. **FLOWERS:** green, many in 1–3" (2.5–7.5 cm) long, loose axial clusters, about ⅛" (3 mm) wide, with 5 tiny rounded petals. **PLANT:** woody vine, up to 20' (6 m) or more long; leaves alternate, compound with 3 leaflets; leaflets ovate, margins entire or with a few large teeth, green. **HABITAT:** swamps, woodlands, and roadsides. **COMMENTS:** *contact with any part of this plant may cause severe dermatitis.*

Angelica

- *Angelica atropurpurea* L.
- Carrot family **Apiaceae**

FLOWERING SEASON: mid June to early July. **FLOWERS:** pale green to greenish white, many in spherical terminal clusters up to 10" (25 cm) wide; individual flowers minute, with 5 tiny petals. **PLANT:** 4–6' (1.2–1.8 m) tall; leaves alternate, with several pinnately compound divisions; leaflets ovate with pointed tips, margins toothed, green; stem purple. **HABITAT:** swamps and moist meadows.

LEAVES WHORLED, COMPOUND

Ginseng

- *Panax quinquefolius* L.
- Ginseng family **Araliaceae**

FLOWERING SEASON: late June to mid-July. **FLOWERS:** yellowish green, 6 to 20 in a small, rounded terminal cluster, about ¹⁄₁₆" (1.6 mm) wide, with 5 inconspicuous petals and 5 prominent stamens. **PLANT:** 8–15" (20–37.5 cm) tall; leaves 3, whorled about the stem, palmately compound with 5 leaflets; leaflets ovate with a pointed tip, margins irregularly toothed, green. **HABITAT:** woodlands. **COMMENTS:** *commercially exploited. Do not disturb.*

FLOWERS SYMMETRICAL, WITH 6 PETALS OR PETAL-LIKE PARTS

LEAVES ALTERNATE, SIMPLE

Carrion-flower

- *Smilax herbacea* L.
- Greenbrier family **Smilacaceae**

FLOWERING SEASON: June. **FLOWERS:** green, many, in rounded, long-stemmed axial clusters, about ⅜" (9 cm) wide, with 6 narrowly lance-shaped, petal-like divisions and several conspicuous, filamentous, white-tipped stamens; unpleasantly fragrant. **PLANT:** climbing vine, 3–6' (0.9–1.8 m) long; leaves alternate on a smooth herbaceous stem, simple, ovate, often with a slightly heart-shaped base, margin entire, green. **HABITAT:** woodlands, thickets, and along waterways. **COMMENTS:** the common name refers to the flowers' odor of rotten meat. Other *Smilax* species have armed woody stems: the stem of the bristly greenbrier, *Smilax hispida*, is covered with numerous tiny prickles; the stem of horse-brier, *Smilax rotundifolia*, has fewer thorns, which are stout, flattened, and rose-like.

False Hellebore

- *Veratrum viride* Ait.
- Lily family **Liliaceae**

FLOWERING SEASON: mid-June to mid-July. **FLOWERS:** yellowish green, many in an 8–24" (20–60 cm) branching terminal cluster, up to 1" (2.5 cm) wide, perianth with 6 oblong, petal-like parts. **PLANT:** 2–8' (0.6–2.4 m) tall; leaves alternate, simple, broadly oval, margin entire, green. **HABITAT:** swamps and wet woods.

Carrion-flower / *Smilax herbacea*

False Hellebore / *Veratrum viride*

Poison Ivy / *Toxicodendron radicans*

Angelica / *Angelica atropurpurea*

Ginseng / *Panax quinquefolius*

FLOWERS NOT RADIALLY SYMMETRICAL; FLOWERS MINUTE, FILAMENTOUS, TUBULAR WITH NO PETAL-LIKE LOBES, OR WITH NO OBVIOUS PETAL-LIKE PARTS

LEAVES BASAL, SIMPLE

Narrow-leaf Cattail
• *Typha angustifolia* L.
• Cattail family **Typhaceae**
FLOWERING SEASON: June. **FLOWERS:** yellowish green, many on a 6–24" (15–61 cm) tall 2-sectioned slender cylindrical terminal spike, staminate flowers on the upper section; pistillate flowers on the lower sections; individual flowers tiny. **PLANT:** 4–8' (1.2–2.4 m) tall; leaves basal, simple, very long and narrow, margin entire, green. **HABITAT:** marshes, edges of ponds, lakes, creeks and rivers, and moist soil. **COMMENTS:** the common cattail, broad-leaf cattail, *Typha latifolia,* is very similar but has broader leaves and a broader terminal spike.

Loesel's Twayblade
• *Liparis loeselii* (L.) L. Rich.
• Orchid family **Orchidaceae**
FLOWERING SEASON: late June through mid-July. **FLOWERS:** yellowish green, 2 to 12 in a loose, slender terminal cluster, about ⅜" (10 mm) tall, with 5 very narrow petals and sepals and an oblong lip. **PLANT:** 2–8" (5–20 cm) tall; leaves 2, basal, simple, oblong, margin entire, green. **HABITAT:** moist soils (from fens to roadside ditches).

Sweetflag, Calamus
• *Acorus americanus* (Raf.) Raf.
• Arum family **Araceae**
FLOWERING SEASON: late May through June. **FLOWERS:** yellowish green, minute, many clustered on a 2–3½" (5–8.8 cm) long, finger-like projection found on the lower third of a leaf-like flower stem.

PLANT: 2–6' (0.6–1.8 m) tall; leaves basal, simple, long and narrow, margin entire, pale green. **HABITAT:** swamps, moist meadows, and along streams.

Arrowleaf, Tuckahoe, Arrow Arum
• *Peltandra virginica* (L.) Schott ex Schott & Endl.
• Arum family **Araceae**
FLOWERING SEASON: mid-June to mid-July. **FLOWERS:** minute, many on an erect cylindrical spike almost entirely enclosed in a green 4–8" (10–20 cm) tall sheath that appears like a rolled up leaf. **PLANT:** 6–30" (15–75 cm) tall; leaves basal, simple, arrowhead-shaped and long-stemmed, margin entire, green. **HABITAT:** swamps, drainage ditches, edges of ponds and lakes, often in standing water.

LEAVES BASAL, COMPOUND OR DEEPLY DIVIDED

Jack-in-the-pulpit
• *Arisaema triphyllum* (L.) (L.) Schott ex Schott & Endl.
• Arum family **Araceae**
FLOWERING SEASON: May through early June. **FLOWERS:** minute, many clustered on an erect, finger-like projection enclosed by a leaf-like sheath; sheath appearing tubular at the base, the upper portion arching forward over the flowering spike; green, usually with purple stripes. **PLANT:** 10–36" (25–90 cm) tall; leaves 1 or 2, basal, long-stalked, each with 3 leaflets; leaflets broadly lance-shaped, margins entire, green. **HABITAT:** woodlands.

Narrow-leaf Cattail / *Typha angustifolia*

Sweetflag, Calamus / *Acorus americanus*

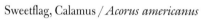

Loesel's Twayblade / *Liparis loeselii*

Jack-in-the-pulpit / *Arisaema triphyllum*

Arrowleaf, Tuckahoe, Arrow Arum / *Peltandra virginica*

Green Dragon, Dragon-root
•*Arisaema dracontium* (L.)
 (L.) Schott ex Schott & Endl.
•Arum family **Araceae**
FLOWERING SEASON: June. **FLOWERS:** minute, many on an erect 1–2" (2.5–5 cm) long, cylindrical yellowish green spike tapering upward another 7" (17.5 cm) above the flowering portion, the lower portion enclosed in a leaf-like sheath. **PLANT:** 8–32" (20–80 cm) tall; leaf usually solitary, basal, long-stalked, with 5 to 17 leaflets in the upper portion, which is usually oriented parallel to the ground; leaflets mostly arranged on the same side of the stalk, oblong, margins entire, green. **HABITAT:** moist woodlands and along streams.

LEAVES ALTERNATE, SIMPLE

Frost Grape
•*Vitis riparia* Michx.
•Grape family **Vitaceae**
FLOWERING SEASON: June. **FLOWERS:** pale green, many in loose axial clusters about 3" (7.5 cm) long; individual flowers minute. **PLANT:** woody vine, up to 25' (7.5 m) or more long; leaves alternate, simple, broadly ovate with 3 to 7 lobes, margin coarsely toothed, green, smooth on both surfaces. **HABITAT:** hedgerows, woodlands, and riverbanks. **COMMENTS:** fox grape, *Vitis lambrusca*, which has many cultivated varieties, has broader leaves with a densely pubescent lower surface.

Clotbur, Common Cocklebur
•*Xanthium strumarium* L.
•Aster family **Asteraceae**
FLOWERING SEASON: mid-August to September. **FLOWERS:** green, minute, enclosed in oblong ½–¾" (1.3–2 cm) long burrs; burr covered with many slender hooked prickles and tipped with 2 beak-like structures. **PLANT:** 1–6' (0.3–1.8 m) tall; leaves alternate, simple, broad and maple-like, margin toothed, green. **HABITAT:** waste areas.

Small Solomon's Seal
•*Polygonatum biflorum* (Walt.) Ell.
•Lily family **Liliaceae**
FLOWERING SEASON: late May to early June. **FLOWERS:** yellowish green, several, found singly or in pairs (occasionally in groups of 3 or 4) in axils, about ½" (1.3 cm) long, tubularly bell-shaped with 6 small pointed teeth, pendant. **PLANT:** 8–36" (20–90 cm) long, leaves alternate, simple, broadly lance-shaped, margin entire, green. **HABITAT:** woodlands. **COMMENTS:** hairy Solomon's Seal, *Polygonatum pubescens*, has hairy veins on the underside of the leaves. *Polygonatum biflorum* has smooth veins.

Helleborine Orchid
•*Epipactis helleborine* (L.) Crantz
•Orchid family **Orchidaceae**
FLOWERING SEASON: mid-July through late August. **FLOWERS:** pale to olive-green with reddish brown tints, 15 to 35 or more in a slender terminal cluster, about ⅗" (15 cm) tall and wide, with 5 broadly lance-shaped, petal-like parts and a cup-shaped lip. **PLANT:** 10–24" (25–60 cm) or more tall; leaves alternate, simple, broadly lance-shaped, margin entire, green. **HABITAT:** woodlands.

Clotbur, Common Cocklebur / *Xanthium strumarium*

Green Dragon, Dragon-root / *Arisaema dracontium*

Helleborine Orchid / *Epipactis helleborine*

Frost Grape / *Vitis riparia*

Small Solomon's Seal / *Polygonatum biflorum*

LEAVES ALTERNATE, COMPOUND OR DEEPLY DIVIDED

Common Mugwort, Wormwood
•*Artemisia vulgaris* L.
•Aster family **Asteraceae**
FLOWERING SEASON: late August through September. **FLOWERHEADS**: greenish, many in the upper leaf axils, individual flowerheads about ³⁄₁₆" (5 mm) wide, oblong. **PLANT**: 1–3½' (0.3–1.1 m) tall; leaves alternate, pinnately compound into sharply toothed lobes, margins coarsely toothed, dark green above, white and densely tomentose beneath. **HABITAT**: waste areas.

LEAVES ALTERNATE AND OPPOSITE ON THE SAME PLANT, DEEPLY DIVIDED

Ragweed
•*Ambrosia artemisiifolia* L.
•Aster family **Asteraceae**
FLOWERING SEASON: mid-August to mid-September. **FLOWERHEADS**: yellowish green, many, in 1–6" (2.5–15 cm) long, slender terminal and upper axial clusters, individual flowerheads about ³⁄₁₆" (5 mm) wide. **PLANT**: 1–6' (0.3–1.8 m) tall; upper leaves alternate, lower leaves mostly opposite, simple, oblong to lance-shaped, margin deeply pinnately cleft and coarsely toothed, green. **HABITAT**: fields, roadsides, and waste areas.

LEAVES OPPOSITE OR WHORLED, SIMPLE

Small Whorled Pogonia
•*Isotria medeoloides* (Pursh) Rafinesque
•Orchid family **Orchidaceae**
FLOWERING SEASON: late May-June. **FLOWERS**: green, solitary or 2, terminal, about 1¼" (3 cm) tall, center of flower appearing tubular and about ¾" (2 cm) long, framed by 3 narrow petal-like sepals. **PLANT**: 8–10" (20–25 cm) tall; leaves 5–6 in a single whorl, simple, broadly lance-shaped, margin entire, green. **HABITAT**: moist woods. **COMMENTS**: *endangered. Do not disturb*. Often overlooked due to the inconspicuous coloration. Report any sightings to the State Conservation Department.

Large Whorled Pogonia
•*Isotria verticillata* (Muhl. ex Willd.) Raf.
•Orchid family **Orchidaceae**
FLOWERING SEASON: late May through early June. **FLOWER**: greenish yellow, solitary, terminal, about 2¾" (6.9 cm) tall, center of flower appearing tubular, about ¾" (1.9 cm) long, framed by 3 very long and narrow brownish sepals. **PLANT**: 5–12" (12.5–30 cm) tall; leaves 5 or 6 in a single whorl, simple, broadly lance-shaped, margin entire, green. **HABITAT**: damp to dry woodlands and swampy edges of fens. **COMMENTS**: Within the area covered by this book, this species may now be limited to a large colony in western Vermont. An attempt to locate a reported population in southern New Hampshire was not successful, although it should be noted that this species does not reliably appear every year.

Stinging Nettle
•*Urtica dioica* L.
•Nettle family **Urticaceae**
FLOWERING SEASON: August-September. **FLOWERS**: pale green, many in long, very slender axial clusters, (about as long as nearby leaves), minute. **PLANT**: 2–7' (0.6–2.1 m) tall; leaves opposite, simple, narrowly ovate to lance-shaped with a rounded to slightly heart-shaped base, sharply toothed, green. **HABITAT**: fields, farmyards, waste areas, and swamps. **COMMENTS**: beware of touching. Nettles are covered with numerous tiny but maddeningly stinging hairs. Wood-

Common Mugwort, Wormwood / *Artemisia vulgaris*

Ragweed / *Ambrosia artemisiifolia*

Small Whorled Pogonia / *Isotria medeoloides*

Large Whorled Pogonia / *Isotria verticillata*

Stinging Nettle / *Urtica dioica*

nettle, *Laportea canadensis*, is the only stinging nettle with alternate leaves. It has broad, ovate leaves and broad, spreading flower clusters; it is found in rich, moist woodlands.

LEAVES OPPOSITE OR WHORLED, COMPOUND

Wild Sarsaparilla
•*Aralia nudicaulis* L.
•Ginseng family **Araliaceae**

FLOWERING SEASON: mid-May to mid-June. **FLOWERS:** greenish, many, on each of usually 3 circular clusters arising from a single stalk, about ⅛" (3 mm) wide, inconspicuous. **PLANT:** 12–15" (30–45 cm) tall; leaf solitary, basal, divided so as to appear as 3 whorled, pinnately compound leaves; leaflets usually 5 per section, of unequal size, ovate with a pointed tip, margins toothed, green. **HABITAT:** woodlands.

Wild Sarsaparilla / *Aralia nudicaulis*

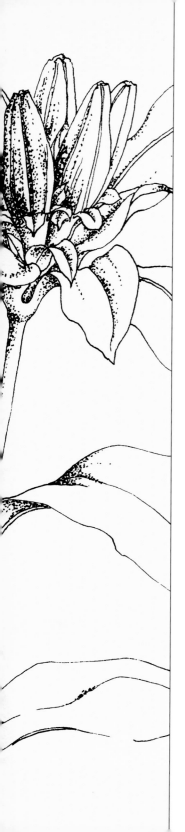

PART FIVE

BLUE TO VIOLET FLOWERS
INCLUDING BLUISH PURPLE

FLOWERS SYMMETRICAL, WITH 3 PETALS OR PETAL-LIKE PARTS

LEAVES BASAL, SIMPLE

Wild Iris, Blue Flag, Fleur-de-lis
- *Iris versicolor* L.
- Iris family **Iridaceae**

FLOWERING SEASON: June through early July. **FLOWERS:** violet-blue, several terminal on an upright stem, about 3" (7.5 cm) wide, perianth 6-parted, 3 outer parts broadly paddle-shaped with downturned tips and yellow and white veining, 3 inner parts smaller, narrower, somewhat erect. **PLANT:** 2–3' (60–90 cm) tall; leaves basal, simple, long and narrow, margin entire, bluish green. **HABITAT:** marshes, wet meadows, and along bodies of water. **COMMENTS:** because most individuals focus on the 3 prominent downturned petals and tend not to notice the 3 less conspicuous upright petals, we have placed this wildflower in this section.

FLOWERS SYMMETRICAL, WITH 4 PETALS OR PETAL-LIKE PARTS

LEAVES OPPOSITE, SIMPLE

Fringed Gentian
- *Gentianopsis crinita* (Froel.) Ma
- Gentian family **Gentianaceae**

FLOWERING SEASON: September-October. **FLOWERS:** blue, several, terminal, about 2" (5 cm) long, tubular with 4 rounded, heavily fringed, apical petal-like lobes. **PLANT:** about 1–3' (30–90 cm) tall; leaves opposite, simple, lance-shaped with a rounded base, margin entire, green. **HABITAT:** moist meadows and roadsides.

Bluets
- *Houstonia caerulea* L.
- Madder family **Rubiaceae**

FLOWERING SEASON: early May to mid-June. **FLOWERS:** pale violet to white with a yellow center, few to several, terminal, about ⁷⁄₁₆" (1.1 cm) wide, tubular with 4 sharply pointed, petal-like lobes. **PLANT:** 3–7" (7.5–17.5 cm) tall; leaves basal and opposite, simple, narrowly paddle-shaped, margin entire, green. **HABITAT:** open grassy areas, often at higher elevations.

Corn Speedwell
- *Veronica arvensis* L.
- Figwort family **Scrophulariaceae**

FLOWERING SEASON: March-September. **FLOWERS:** blue or sometimes bluish white, several to numerous, axial, ¹⁄₁₆–¹⁄₈" (1.5–3 mm) wide, tubular at the base, with 4 tiny, somewhat unequal, rounded petal-like lobes. **PLANT:** 3–10" (7.5–25 cm) tall, often prostrate when growing in lawns; leaves opposite, simple, ovate to oval, margin toothed or sometimes entire; green. **HABITAT:** fields, lawns, woods, and waste areas.

FLOWERS SYMMETRICAL, WITH 5 PETALS OR PETAL-LIKE PARTS

LEAVES ALTERNATE, SIMPLE

Forget-me-not
- *Myosotis scorpioides* L.
- Borage family **Boraginaceae**

FLOWERING SEASON: May-July. **FLOWERS:** pale blue with a yellow center, many, in long, slender clusters, about ¼" (6 mm) wide, with 5 nearly round, petal-like lobes. **PLANT:** 6–18" (15–45 cm) tall; leaves alternate, simple, oblong, minutely hairy, margin entire, green. **HABITAT:** along brooks, marshes, and drainage ditches.

Bluets / *Houstonia caerulea*

Wild Iris, Blue Flag, Fleur-de-lis / *Iris versicolor*

Corn Speedwell / *Veronica arvensis*

Fringed Gentian / *Gentianopsis crinita*

Forget-me-not / *Myosotis scorpioides*

Creeping Bellflower
•*Campanula rapunculoides* L.
•Bluebell family **Campanulaceae**
FLOWERING SEASON: late June to early August. FLOWERS: blue to violet, many in a slender 1-sided terminal cluster, about 1¼" (3.1 cm) long, bell-shaped with 5 somewhat flaring triangular lobes. PLANT: about 1–3' (30–90 cm) tall; leaves alternate, simple, broadly lance-shaped, margin toothed, green. HABITAT: fields, roadsides, and waste areas.

Harebell, Bluebell
•*Campanula rotundifolia* L.
•Bluebell family **Campanulaceae**
FLOWERING SEASON: late June through August. FLOWERS: blue, few to several, in slender 1-sided upper axial clusters, up to 1" (2.5 cm) long, bell-shaped with 5 triangular lobes. PLANT: 6–39" (15–97.5 cm) or more tall; leaves basal and alternate, simple, basal leaves broadly heart-shaped; stem leaves very narrow, green. HABITAT: moist rocky areas.

LEAVES ALTERNATE, DEEPLY LOBED

Nightshade
•*Solanum dulcamara* L.
•Nightshade family **Solanaceae**
FLOWERING SEASON: early June into August. FLOWERS: purple, blue, or white with a protruding yellow center, several, in loose clusters, about ½" (1.3 cm) wide, corolla with 5 deeply recurved, sharply pointed, petal-like lobes, often nodding. PLANT: vine-like, 2–8' (0.6–2.4 m) long; leaves alternate, simple, 3-lobed, central lobe large, broadly tear-shaped, lateral lobes small and lance-shaped, margin entire, green; fruit green to bright red when ripe, tomato-like, *poisonous*. HABI-

TAT: roadsides, waste areas, and thickets.
COMMENTS: often found with flowers and fruit simultaneously.

LEAVES OPPOSITE, SIMPLE

Common Periwinkle
•*Vinca minor* L.
•Dogbane family **Apocynaceae**
FLOWERING SEASON: late April through May. FLOWERS: blue or occasionally white or pinkish, few, solitary in axils, about 1" (2.5 cm) wide, with 5 wide, blunt, petal-like parts. PLANT: prostrate, stems 6–24" (15–60 cm) long; leaves opposite, simple, oblong, margin entire, green. HABITAT: escaped from cultivation into woodlands and meadows.

Blue Phlox
•*Phlox divaricata* L.
•Phlox family **Polemoniaceae**
FLOWERING SEASON: mid-May to mid-June. FLOWERS: blue, several to many in a rounded terminal cluster, about 1" (2.5 cm) wide, tubular, with 5 paddle-shaped, petal-like lobes. PLANT: 12–20" (30–50 cm) tall; leaves opposite, simple, lance-shaped, margin entire, green. HABITAT: woodlands.

Blue Vervain
•*Verbena hastata* L.
•Verbena family **Verbenaceae**
FLOWERING SEASON: July through early September. FLOWERS: blue, many, in slender terminal clusters, about ⅛" (3 mm) wide, tubular with 5 tiny lobes. PLANT: 3–7' (0.9–2.1 m) tall; leaves opposite, simple, lance-shaped, margin toothed, green. HABITAT: moist fields, meadows, and drainage ditches.

Harebell, Bluebell / *Campanula rotundifolia*

Creeping Bellflower / *Campanula rapunculoides*

Nightshade / *Solanum dulcamara*

Blue Vervain / *Verbena hastata*

Blue Phlox / *Phlox divaricata*

Common Periwinkle / *Vinca minor*

FLOWERS SYMMETRICAL, WITH 6 PETALS OR PETAL-LIKE PARTS

LEAVES BASAL, SIMPLE

Blue-eyed Grass
- *Sisyrinchium angustifolium* Mill.
- Iris family **Iridaceae**

FLOWERING SEASON: late May through June. FLOWERS: violet-blue with a yellow center, 1 to 3, terminal on an upright 2-edged stem, about ¾" (1.9 cm) wide, perianth with 6 oblong, bristle-tipped, petal-like parts. PLANT: 3–14" (7.5–35 cm) tall; leaves basal, simple, long and narrow, margin entire, green, flowering stem with a long, leaf-like bract halfway up the stem. HABITAT: moist fields and meadows.

FLOWERS SYMMETRICAL, WITH 7 OR MORE PETALS OR PETAL-LIKE PARTS

LEAVES ALTERNATE, SIMPLE

Chicory
- *Cichorium intybus* L.
- Aster family **Asteraceae**

FLOWERING SEASON: mid-June to mid-September. FLOWERHEADS: blue or occasionally white; many, in clusters of 1 to 4 along the branching stems, individual flowerheads about 1¼" (3.1 cm) wide, rimmed with many oblong, minutely 5-toothed, petal-like rays. PLANT: 1–3' (30–90 cm) tall; leaves basal and alternate, simple, lance-shaped, margin unevenly toothed, green. HABITAT: fields, roadsides, and waste areas.

Blue Wood Aster
- *Aster cordifolius* L.
- Aster family **Asteraceae**

FLOWERING SEASON: September-October. FLOWERHEADS: white, violet, or blue, with a pinkish to purplish center, many, terminal and upper axial, individual flowerheads ½–¾" (1.3–1.9 cm) wide, rimmed with 10 to 20 petal-like rays. PLANT: 1–5' (0.3–1.5 m) tall; leaves alternate and basal; upper leaves lance-shaped; lower and basal leaves heart-shaped with a deeply cleft base, margin toothed, green. HABITAT: woods and thickets.

FLOWERS NOT RADIALLY SYMMETRICAL; FLOWERS MINUTE, FILAMENTOUS, TUBULAR WITH NO PETAL-LIKE LOBES, OR WITH NO OBVIOUS PETAL-LIKE PARTS

LEAVES BASAL, SIMPLE

Pickerel-weed
- *Pontederia cordata* L.
- Pickerel-weed family **Pontederiaceae**

FLOWERING SEASON: late July-August. FLOWERS: blue, many on a densely flowered 1–3" (2.5–7.5 cm) long, cylindrical terminal cluster, about ½" (1.3 cm) wide, perianth tubular and 2-lipped, each lip with 3 long, petal-like lobes, the central lip of the upper lobe with 2 large yellow spots. PLANT: 1–4' (0.3–1.2 m) tall; leaves mostly basal, simple, narrowly heart-shaped, margin entire, green. HABITAT: aquatic, in the shallow borders of ponds and streams.

Great Spurred Violet, Selkirk Violet
- *Viola selkirkii* Pursh ex Goldie
- Violet family **Violaceae**

FLOWERING SEASON: May. FLOWERS: violet, several, on individual stalks, about ½" (1.3 cm) wide, with 5 unequal rounded petals and a thick, blunt spur at the base. PLANT: 1½–4" (3.8–10 cm) tall; leaves basal, simple, broadly ovate to nearly round with a deeply cleft, heart-shaped base, margin finely toothed, green. HABITAT: moist woodlands.

Blue Wood Aster / *Aster cordifolius*

Great Spurred Violet, Selkirk Violet / *Viola selkirkii*

Blue-eyed Grass / *Sisyrinchium angustifolium*

Pickerel-weed / *Pontederia cordata*

Chicory / *Cichorium intybus*

LEAVES ALTERNATE, SIMPLE

Long-spurred Violet

Viola rostrata Pursh
Violet family **Violaceae**

FLOWERING SEASON: May. **FLOWERS:** pale violet with blue veining, several, terminal, about ¾" (1.9 cm) wide, with 5 unequal rounded petals and a long, slender spur at the base. **PLANT:** 2–7" (5–17.5 cm) tall; leaves basal and alternate, simple, somewhat heart-shaped, margin toothed, green. **HABITAT:** woodlands.

Viper's Bugloss

•*Echium vulgare* L.
•Borage family **Boraginaceae**

FLOWERING SEASON: mid-June to mid-August. **FLOWERS:** bright blue to purplish, several to many in tall, slender clusters, up to 1" (2.5 cm) long, tubular with 5 unequal rounded lobes. **PLANT:** 12–30" (30–75 cm) tall; leaves alternate, simple, narrowly oblong, hairy, margin entire, green. **HABITAT:** fields and waste areas.

Virginia Blue Bells, Virginia Cowslip

•*Mertensia virginica* (L.) Pers. ex Link
•Borage family **Boraginaceae**

FLOWERING SEASON: mid-April to mid-May. **FLOWERS:** pale blue to bluish purple, several to many, in terminal clusters, about 1" (2.5 cm) long, trumpet-shaped, usually nodding. **PLANT:** 1–2' (30–60 cm) tall; leaves alternate, simple, oval, margin entire, green. **HABITAT:** moist meadows and woodlands.

Blue Toadflax

•*Linaria canadensis* (L.) Dumort
•Figwort family **Scrophulariaceae**

FLOWERING SEASON: May-September **FLOWERS:** pale blue, several to many, alternate in a slender terminal cluster, about ¼" (6 mm) long, tubular and 2-lipped with a hook-shaped slender spur at the base; upper lip with 2 erect, petal-like lobes; lower lip with 3 larger, spreading, petal-like lobes. **PLANT:** 4–26" (10–65 cm) tall; leaves alternate, simple, long and narrow, margin entire, green. **HABITAT:** dry, often sandy, soil.

Dwarf Snapdragon

•*Chaenorrhinum minus* (L.) Lange
•Figwort family **Scrophulariaceae**

FLOWERING SEASON: July-August. **FLOWERS:** lilac to pale blue, many, individual flowers in leaf axils, about ¼" (6 mm) long, tubular with a basal spur and 2 lips; upper lip 2-lobed, lower lip 3-lobed. **PLANT:** 6–12" (15–31 cm) tall; leaves alternate, simple, narrowly oblong, margin entire, green. **HABITAT:** waste areas.

Great Blue Lobelia

•*Lobelia siphilitica* L.
•Bluebell family **Campanulaceae**

FLOWERING SEASON: August-September. **FLOWERS:** bright blue, several to many in a showy slender terminal cluster, up to 1" (2.5 cm) long, tubular at the base, with 3 broad lower lobes and 2 smaller upper lobes. **PLANT:** 1–3' (30–90 cm) tall; leaves alternate, simple, lance-shaped, margin toothed, green. **HABITAT:** moist meadows, swamps, and edges of large bodies of water.

Virginia Blue Bells, Virginia Cowslip / *Mertensia virginica*

Great Blue Lobelia / *Lobelia siphilitica*

Viper's Bugloss / *Echium vulgare*

Blue Toadflax / *Linaria canadensis*

Long-spurred Violet / *Viola rostrata*

Dwarf Snapdragon / *Chaenorrhinum minus*

Spiked Lobelia

•*Lobelia spicata* Lam.
•Bluebell family **Campanulaceae**
FLOWERING SEASON: July-August. FLOW-ERS: pale blue, many in a slender terminal cluster, about ⁵⁄₁₆" (8 mm) long, tubular and 2-lipped; upper lip with 2 narrow, erect lobes; lower lip with 3 larger, lance-shaped lobes. PLANT: 1–4' (0.3–1.2 m) tall; leaves alternate and basal, simple, oblong to oval, margin wavy, green. HABITAT: sandy soil along woodlands and roadsides. COMMENTS: brook lobelia, *Lobelia kalmii*, found in moist soils along waterways, is pale blue with a white central area on the lower lip. Water lobelia, *L. dortmanna*, which grows in shallow water, has pale blue or whitish flowers and small basal leaves that are frequently submerged.

LEAVES ALTERNATE, COMPOUND

Blue Columbine

•*Aquilegia vulgaris* L.
•Crowfoot family **Ranunculaceae**
FLOWERING SEASON: June. FLOWERS: blue to purple, one to several, terminal, about 1½" (3.8 cm) long with 5 tubular petals, nodding. PLANT: 1–2' (30–60 cm) tall; leaves alternate, compound with 3 to 9 leaflets; leaflets wedge-shaped and irregularly lobed, green. HABITAT: woodlands, roadsides, and meadows.

Alfalfa

•*Medicago sativa* L.
•Bean family **Fabaceae**
FLOWERING SEASON: June-August. FLOWERS: violet to blue, many, in elongated clusters, about ¼" (6 mm) long, narrowly pea-like. PLANT: 1–2' (30–60 cm) tall; leaves alternate, compound with 3 leaflets; leaflets obovate, margins minutely toothed near the tip, green; fruit a cluster of brown, tightly spiraled pods. HABITAT: fields, meadows, and waste areas.

Cow-vetch

•*Vicia cracca* L.
•Bean family **Fabaceae**
FLOWERING SEASON: mid-June through July. FLOWERS: bluish purple, many, in 1–4" (2.5–10 cm) long, slender, 1-sided axial clusters, up to ½" (1.3 cm) long, narrowly pea-like, slightly nodding. PLANT: trailing vine, 2–4' (0.6–1.2 m) long; leaves alternate, pinnately compound with 18 to 24 leaflets; leaflets narrowly lance-shaped, margins entire, green. HABITAT: fields and waste areas.

Wild Lupine

•*Lupinus perennis* L.
•Bean family **Fabaceae**
FLOWERING SEASON: mid-May to mid-June. FLOWERS: bicolored, blue and white, sometimes pinkish, many in an erect, cylindrical 6–10" (15–25 cm) tall terminal cluster, about ¾" (1.9 cm) long, pea-like. PLANT: 1–2' (30–60 cm) tall; leaves alternate, palmately compound with 7 to 11 leaflets; leaflets narrowly lance-shaped, margins entire, green. HABITAT: dry sandy soil.

LEAVES OPPOSITE, SIMPLE

Bottle Gentian, Closed Gentian

•*Gentiana clausa* Raf.
•Gentian family **Gentianaceae**
FLOWERING SEASON: mid-August to mid-September. FLOWERS: blue, several, usually in a terminal cluster, about 1½" (3.8 cm) long, corolla tubular, club-shaped to bottle-shaped, nearly to completely closed at the tip. PLANT: 1–2' (30–60 cm) tall; leaves usually opposite, often whorled in the upper 2 axils, simple, lance-shaped, margin entire, green. HABITAT: moist meadows and fens.

Cow-vetch / *Vicia cracca*

Wild Lupine / *Lupinus perennis*

Alfalfa / *Medicago sativa*

Blue Columbine / *Aquilegia vulgaris*

Bottle Gentian, Closed Gentian / *Gentiana clausa*

Spiked Lobelia / *Lobelia spicata*

Carpet-bugleweed

•*Ajuga reptans* L.
•Mint family **Lamiaceae**
FLOWERING SEASON: May-June. FLOW-
ERS: blue or nearly white, terminal
flowers several on a short spike, lower
flowers several in axial clusters, about
½" (1.3 cm) long, tubular with 2 lips;
upper lip short, truncate; lower lip 3-
lobed. PLANT: 6–15" (15–38 cm) tall;
leaves opposite and sessile on a square
stem, simple, oblong to elliptical, margin
bluntly toothed to nearly entire, green.
HABITAT: fields, moist woodlands, and
often a weed in flower gardens.

Common Skullcap

•*Scutellaria galericulata* L.
•Mint family **Lamiaceae**
FLOWERING SEASON: July-August. FLOW-
ERS: blue, several, in pairs in axils, about
1" (2.5 cm) long, tubular, 2-lipped;
upper lip hood-like and arched over the
lower lip. PLANT: 1–3' (30–90 cm) tall;
leaves opposite on a square stem, simple,
lance-shaped, margin toothed, green.
HABITAT: swamps and along streams.
COMMENTS: 9 species of skullcaps have
been reported from this region. Mad-dog
skullcap, *Scutellaria lateriflora*, bears
flowers in long, narrow axial clusters.

Gill-over-the-ground

•*Glechoma hederacea* L.
•Mint family **Lamiaceae**
FLOWERING SEASON: late April into July.
FLOWERS: blue to violet, several, in axial
clusters, about ¾" (1.9 cm) long, tubular
with 2 lips; upper lip 2-lobed, lower lip
3-lobed. PLANT: prostrate, creeping, up
to 18" (45 cm) long; leaves opposite on
a square stem, simple, kidney-shaped,
margin scalloped, green. HABITAT: waste
areas, woods, thickets, and lawns.

Monkeyflower

•*Mimulus ringens* L.
•Figwort family **Scrophulariaceae**
FLOWERING SEASON: mid-July through
August. FLOWERS: pale violet, few, axial,
about 1" (2.5 cm) long, tubular with 2
spreading lips; upper lip with 2 petal-
like lobes; lower lip with 3 rounded,
petal-like lobes. PLANT: 1–3' (60–90 cm)
tall; leaves opposite on a square stem,
simple, lance-shaped, margin toothed,
green. HABITAT: swamps and along
streams.

Bird's-eye Speedwell

•*Veronica persica* Poir.
•Figwort family **Scrophulariaceae**
FLOWERING SEASON: May-June. FLOW-
ERS: a mixture of white and bluish purple with purple veining, many, axial,
long-stalked, about ⁷⁄₁₆" (1.1 cm) wide,
tubular at the base, with 4 large,
unequal, rounded, petal-like lobes.
PLANT: often prostrate and forming
mats; leaves opposite, simple, ovate,
margin toothed, green. HABITAT: lawns,
fields, and waste areas. COMMENTS:
Veronica chamaedrys, also know as bird's-
eye speedwell, has similar flowers, but
they are borne on spike-like terminal
clusters.

Carpet-bugleweed / *Ajuga reptans*

Gill-over-the-ground / *Glechoma hederacea*

Bird's-eye Speedwell / *Veronica persica*

Common Skullcap / *Scutellaria galericulata*

Monkeyflower / *Mimulus ringens*

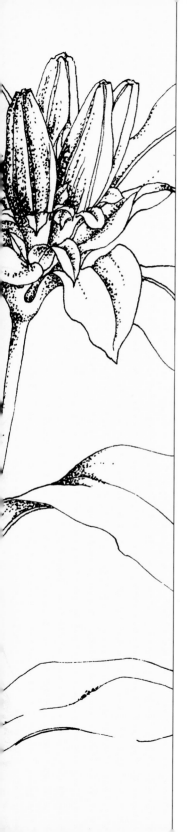

PART SIX

DARK PURPLE
TO BROWN FLOWERS

FLOWERS SYMMETRICAL, WITH 3-4 PETALS OR PETAL-LIKE PARTS

TYPICAL LEAVES LACKING, PARASITIC ON BLACK SPRUCE

Dwarf Mistletoe
•*Arceuthobium pusillum* C. Peck
•Mistletoe family **Viscaceae**
FLOWERING SEASON: late April through early June. **FLOWERS**: brown to greenish brown, many, solitary or paired in axils; dioecious (male and female flowers different, in this species typically found on separate host trees); male flowers about ⅛" (3 mm) wide; female flowers tiny, much smaller than the scale-like leaves; male flowers as large or larger than the scale-like leaves, with 3–4 (occasionally 2) pointed, petal-like divisions, with a bright yellow stamen at the base of each petal-like part. **PLANT**: parasitic, usually on twigs of black spruce; stem ⅛–¾" (3–19 mm) long; leaves simple, scale-like, nearly round, tiny, tightly appressed to the stem, greenish brown. **HABITAT**: fens and bogs. **COMMENTS**: a black spruce, *Picea mariana*, infected with dwarf mistletoe, has much denser foliage than an uninfected tree.

FLOWERS SYMMETRICAL, WITH 3 PETALS OR PETAL-LIKE PARTS

LEAVES BASAL, SIMPLE

Wild Ginger
•*Asarum canadense* L.
•Birthwort family **Aristolochiaceae**
FLOWERING SEASON: late April through May. **FLOWER**: brownish purple, solitary, axial, about 1" (2.5 cm) wide, tubular with 3 narrowly triangular, petal-like lobes, lying on or just above the ground. **PLANT**: 6–12" (15–30 cm) tall; leaves

paired, appearing basal, simple, kidney-shaped with a pointed tip, long-stalked, margin entire, green. **HABITAT**: woodlands.

FLOWERS SYMMETRICAL, WITH 6 PETALS OR PETAL-LIKE PARTS

LEAVES OPPOSITE, COMPOUND

Blue Cohosh
•*Caulophyllum thalictroides* (L.) Michx.
•Barberry family **Berberidaceae**
FLOWERING SEASON: mid-April into May. **FLOWERS**: greenish purple, brownish purple, or yellowish green, several in a loosely flowered cluster, up to ½" (1.3 cm) wide, with 6 petal-like sepals. **PLANT**: 1–3' (30–90 cm) tall; leaves opposite with 3 pinnately compound sections; leaflets oval, 3 to 5 lobes, margin entire, green. **HABITAT**: woodlands.

FLOWERS NOT RADIALLY SYMMETRICAL; FLOWERS MINUTE, OR WITH NO OBVIOUS PETAL-LIKE PARTS

TYPICAL LEAVES LACKING

Spotted Coralroot
•*Corallorhiza maculata* (Raf.) Raf.
•Orchid family **Orchidaceae**
FLOWERING SEASON: late July through August. **FLOWERS**: greenish purple and white with purple spots, 10 to 30 in a slender terminal cluster on a purplish to brownish stem, about ½" (1.3 cm) tall and wide, with 5 greenish purple petals and sepals and a white, purple-spotted lip. **PLANT**: 8–16" (20–40 cm) tall; leaves lacking. **HABITAT**: woodlands. **COMMENTS**: coralroots are indirect parasites that feed on other plants. Early coralroot, *Corallorhiza trifida*, which blooms in

Dwarf Mistletoe / *Arceuthobium pusillum*

Black Spruce on right, infected by *Arceutho-bium pusillium*; uninfected tree on left

Blue Cohosh / *Caulophyllum thalictroides*

Wild Ginger / *Asarum canadense*

Spotted Coralroot / *Corallorhiza maculata*

June, is the only species with predominantly green coloration. The autumn coralroot, *Corallorhiza odontorhiza*, which blooms in late August through September, has tiny ⅛" (3 mm) flowers that rarely open fully.

LEAVES BASAL, SIMPLE

Skunk-cabbage
• *Symplocarpus foetidus* (L.) Salisb. ex Nutt.
• Arum family **Araceae**
FLOWERING SEASON: March-April. **FLOWERS:** minute, many on a globular cluster enclosed in a stiff 3–6" (7.5–15 cm) tall, firm, hood-shaped sheath that is purple-brown to greenish yellow and often mottled. **PLANT:** 1–2' (30–60 cm) tall; leaves basal, large, simple, broad with protruding veins like those of a cabbage, margin entire, green; unpleasant odor if bruised. **HABITAT:** swamps, moist soil. **COMMENTS:** the flowers, which emerge before the leaves, sometimes bloom through the snow.

LEAVES ALTERNATE, COMPOUND

Groundnut
• *Apios americana* Medik.
• Bean family **Fabaceae**
FLOWERING SEASON: August to mid-September. **FLOWERS:** brownish purple, many, in dense axial clusters, about ½" (1.3 cm) long, pea-like; fragrant. **PLANT:** vine-like, 3–8' (0.9–2.4 m) long; leaves alternate, pinnately compound with 5 to 7 leaflets; leaflets ovate, margins entire, green. **HABITAT:** moist thickets and meadows.

Skunk-cabbage / *Symplocarpus foetidus*

Groundnut / *Apios americana*

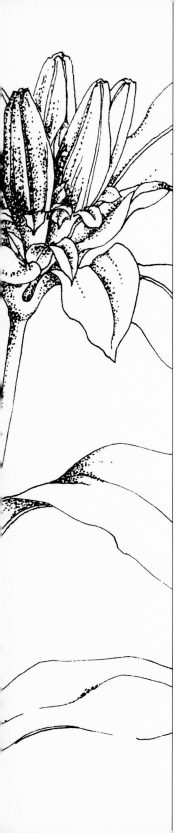

GLOSSARIES AND INDEXES

VISUAL GLOSSARY
GLOSSARY OF TERMS
INDEX OF COMMON NAMES
INDEX OF GENERA
AND SPECIES

❧

VISUAL GLOSSARY

FLORAL PARTS

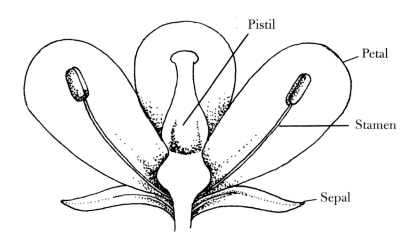

Pistil

Petal

Stamen

Sepal

FLOWER TYPES

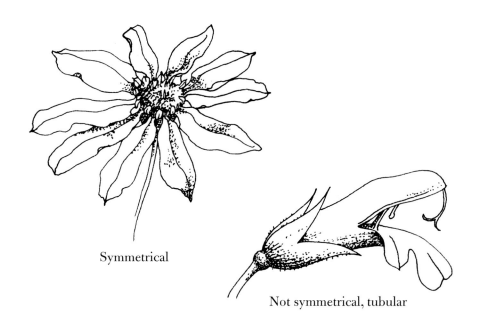

Symmetrical

Not symmetrical, tubular

LEAF TYPES

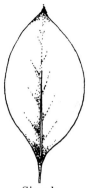

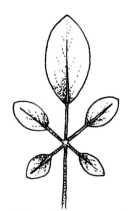

Simple   Pinnately compound   Palmately compound

LEAF PARTS

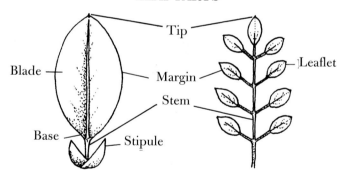

Tip

Blade — Margin —

Leaflet

Stem

Base — Stipule

LEAF ARRANGEMENT

Opposite   Alternate   Whorled   Basal

LEAF MARGINS

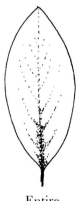
Entire

Toothed

Lobed

LEAF TIPS

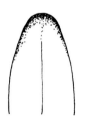
Rounded, blunt

Tapered

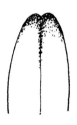
Notched

LEAF AND PETAL BASES

Rounded

Tapered

Heart-shaped

GLOSSARY OF TERMS

ALTERNATE: having leaves arranged singly at different positions along the sides of the stem

APICAL: toward the tip

AXILLARY: located at a leaf-stem juncture

AXIS: the main stem

BASAL: located at the base

BOG: a wet, acidic, nutrient-poor peat land that relies on atmosphere sources for its moisture

BRACT: a small leaf-like structure

CALYX: the basal part of a flower that includes the sepals

COMPOUND: a leaf having two or more leaflets

COROLLA: the apical portion of a flower that includes the petals

DIOECIOUS: having male and female flowers on separate plants

ENDANGERED: referring to species having five or fewer sites, or fewer than 1,000 individuals known in New York State

ENTIRE: having a continuous margin unbroken by indentations or teeth

EVERGREEN: a plant retaining most of the leaves through the winter

FEN: a peatland that receives much of its moisture from ground water sources, typically less acidic and richer in nutrients than a true bog

FERTILE: being capable of sexual reproduction

HERBACEOUS: not woody

LEAFLET: one blade-like part of a compound leaf

LOBE: one part of a leaf or flower that is typically rounded

MARGIN: the edge

NODDING: bending downward

OBLANCEOLATE: pertaining to a leaf that is broadest near the tip

OBLONG: having sides nearly parallel and longer than broad

OBOVATE: egg-shaped, but with the broader end near the tip, the opposite of ovate

OPPOSITE: having leaves arranged in pairs on opposing sides of a stem

OVATE: shaped like an egg, with the broader end at the base

PALMATE: resembling a hand with spread fingers; in a leaf, having divisions radiating out from the center

PENDANT: suspended or hanging down

PERFOLIATE: pertaining to a leaf or leaves with the bases completely surrounding the stem and appearing to be pierced by it

PERIANTH: the combined term for the petals and sepals

PETAL: a usually colorful leaf-like part of the corolla

PINNATE: a leaf with leaflets arranged on opposite sides of the axis, resembling the divisions of a feather

PISTILLATE: referring to either a female flower or the female parts of a complete flower

PROSTRATE: lying flat on the ground

PUBESCENT: coated with short, soft hairs

RAY: the petal-like parts rimming the flowerheads of some species of the Aster family

RECURVED: curved backward or downward

RETICULATION: a net-like pattern

SEPAL: a leaf-like part of the calyx that may be either green or brightly colored

SESSILE: lacking a stalk

SIMPLE: pertaining to a leaf with a single undivided blade

SPATHULATE: shaped like a spoon

SPHERICAL: round or nearly so

SPUR: a tubular extension found on selected flower species, often containing nectar

STAMEN: the male or pollen-producing part of a flower

STAMINATE: referring to either a male flower or the male parts of a complete flower

STEM: the main axis that supports a plant

STERILE: not being capable of sexual reproduction

SWAMP: a wetland area typically containing woody vegetation

TERMINAL: located at the tip

THREATENED: referring to species having 6–19 sites, or fewer than 3,000 individuals known in New York State

TOMENTOSE: having soft matted hairs

TRUNCATE: cut off at one end

VEIN: a small enclosed channel in a leaf or petal through which nutrients and fluids pass

WASTE AREA: unutilized land typically in proximity to human habitation, frequently a site of organic wastes such as lawn clippings

WHORLED: having leaves arranged in groups of three or more around the same point on a stem

INDEX OF COMMON NAMES

INDEX OF GENERA AND SPECIES

ALAN E. BESSETTE is a professor of biology at Utica College of Syracuse University. He is an author of *Wildlfowers of New York State in Color, Plants and Flowers: An Archival Sourcebook, Trees and Shrubs of the Adirondacks, Birds of the Adirondacks,* and several books on mushrooms including *Edible Wild Mushrooms of North America, Mushrooms of North America in Color: A Field Guide Companion to Seldom-Illustrated Fungi,* and *Mushrooms of Northeastern North America*

ARLEEN RAINIS BESSETTE is a mycologist and botanical photographer, as well as a psychologist. She is author of *Wildlfowers of New York State in Color, Taming the Wild Mushroom: A Culinary Guide to Market Foraging, Mushrooms of North America in Color,* and *Mushrooms of Northeastern North America*. Arleen has won several national awards for her photography and teaches courses in mycology for the North American Mycological Association and other organizations.

WILLIAM K. CHAPMAN, a biology teacher and member of the adjunct faculty at Utica College of Syracuse University, is an author of *Wildlfowers of New York State in Color, Orchids of the Northeast, Hickory, Chicory, and Dock* (a wild foods guide), *Plants and Flowers: An Archival Sourcebook, Pheasants under Glass,* and individual field guides to the trees, mammals, and birds of the Adirondacks. He is also a contributing author and photographer for *Deer: The Wildlife Series*. His nature photography has appeared in *National Geographic* and the *New York State Conservationist*.

VALERIE CONLEY CHAPMAN is employed by Utica College of Syracuse University. She is an author of *Wildlfowers of New York State in Color*. Her photography has been published in *Birds of the Adirondacks* and *Mammals of the Adirondacks*. She enjoys travel, hiking, swimming, and beachcombing with her husband and two children, Andy and Carey.

DATE DUE

AUG 0 4 2005